The Commandments

of a

Female Hustler

by

Stacey Fenner

42,000 words

ISBN 978-1532711718

CONTENTS

Dedication..7

Acknowledgements 8

Chapter 1 11

Chapter 2 15

Chapter 3 20

Chapter 4 26

Chapter 5 32

Chapter 6 38

Chapter 7 43

Chapter 8 50

Chapter 9 55

Chapter 10 58

Chapter 11 62

Chapter 12 67

Chapter 13 71

Chapter 14 77

Chapter 15 83

Chapter 16 86

Chapter 17 94

Chapter 18 103

Chapter 19 109

Chapter 20 113

Chapter 21 118

Chapter 22 125

Chapter 23 130

Chapter 24 134

Chapter 25 139

Chapter 26 144

Chapter 27..150

Chapter 28..158

Chapter 29..162

Chapter 30..165

Chapter 31..173

Chapter 32..180

Chapter 33..192

Chapter 34..196

Chapter 35..200

Other Books by Stacey Fenner 204

About the Author 206

Visit Stacey Fenner's Facebook for the latest news and updates.

Instagram: authorstaceyfenner

Twitter: @sfenner1

Facebook: www.facebook.com/authorstaceyfenner

DEDICATION

This book is dedicated to two of the most important women that I will ever have in my life. My grandmother, Aronia Edwards; she would be so proud of me, and my mother, Paulette Fenner. A mother's love can never compare to any other love.

ACKNOWLEDGMENTS

First and foremost, I would like to give the honor to God for giving me the gift to write and an imagination that is limitless.

I have to thank my rocks; my father, Lester Fenner and my mother, Paulette Fenner, for all of their support that they give me day in and day out! I love you both with everything in me. My husband, Keith Blackwell, thank you for putting up with me, especially when I'm so busy writing that I can't even be the wife that you need me to be. I love you! Thank you to my two daughters, Jasmine & Janay, for being so understanding of time not spent because of my dream to be an author. I can't leave out my Nook, my grandson. You stole my heart! Thank you to my brothers, Kirk & Darin Fenner, for your loving support. Thank you to my loving family that supported me and wished me well on my success! It's too many to name, just know I love you all!

Special s/o to Darin for being in Savannah promoting/selling my book, and let's not forget you took A Toxic Love Affair all the way to the Dallas Stadium!

I have to send a special s/o to Shartarra Penn for believing in me enough to invest and see me through on this solo project. You spoke this into existence! I love you!

Thank you to a team of people that ride with me, push with me, cry with me, and put up with me; I couldn't do this without any of you. Gayle Wise, my everything; Michael Lewis, my brother; Erica Cassell, my sister; Safiya Staggers, my cousin…each and every one of you have gone out there, promoted me, and brought back sales! I love my team! I'm so blessed and I thank God daily to have genuine people that are rare and few between that rock and roll for me, not just with me!

Thank you to Facebook for opening up doors for me to network and market myself. I was able to open up doors that I didn't even think was possible! Thank you to Tiffany Lynne, of Gray Publishing, for getting this editing done for me in a timely manner on such short notice. I appreciate you and your work.

CHAPTER 1

GIRLS NIGHT OUT

"What's up Bitches? Are y'all ready to cook up this pussy plan? Y'all ain't been on top of your game! It's time to get your money up. I figured having this little 'girl's night out' would give y'all some motivation to start handling business." I said to my girls Binky and Jay. We been rocking and rolling since we all ended up in the projects of Latrobe.

"La, you are always so extra with everything. Calm it down a little bit!" Binky laughed at me. "Jay and I have been running into some unfortunate situations. We just haven't found our money bag yet." I wanted to tell them to broaden their horizons, and stop always looking for the dope boy. Seniors have money too, but I'll try and let them figure that part out.

"Ladies listen, we are all at that twenty-five mark. It's time to grow into lady status!" Jay strutted her way over to the bar to pour herself a drink. "This is a very nice suite that you got for us La."

"Don't try and play me! You already know everything I do is top of the line. There's no such thing as half-stepping over this way here. Jay, please explain to me what lady status is, because last time I checked, your bank account is at zero. Fuck lady status! This is called getting paid status! Your pussy can't hustle no more; it's broke down or something?" La asked. *Jay must have forgotten who the hell she was talking to.*

"Oh trust me, there's nothing wrong down there. I'm just trying to explore other options that are more suitable for my needs." La replied. *Other options, is this bitch crazy? We don't have any other options. All we've ever known was how to get money by fucking! Point blank, period! I'll let Binky handle this.*

"Really Jay?" Binky and I looked at her like she had ten heads. "It looks like somebody is trying to turn over a new leaf all of a sudden." *Awe shit! Jay is barking up the wrong tree. She better hope Binky don't knock her back into reality.* Bink got that mean left hook; she's the fighter of us three.

"Yes, don't y'all think that we are getting older and it's time to simmer down and at least try to do the right thing?" *Here Jay goes again; she's starting to get on fuckin nerves.*

"The right thing for me and my situation right now is a damn dollar. I don't know what you're talking about, Jay, but me and Lala are on the same page. We look too damn good; got too much ass on us to be walking around here broke. We'll be back on top again as long as you stick to the script. Don't go acting all brand new on us. Tomorrow ain't promised and I'm going to fuck until I die. Even if I make it to the age of eighty, wrinkled and all, I'm going to still be getting it in."

I couldn't help but laugh at Binky and her nasty ass. "That's right girl, I hear that shit! Jay, I see you over there turning your nose up! You better get your mind right!"

"I'm just saying the hustle is getting old. When do we stop? All I been getting is a wet ass and a couple of coins. I want to build with somebody one day. I'm looking to meet my soul mate so we can travel and do things. These broke ass niggas ain't trying to do nothing but travel from the east side to west side…and that's if they do that." *I really wish Jay could hear herself. She must not be working it right; she might need to be re-trained. I have to teach her some new tricks.*

"You have always been the weakest; I should've known that one day you would be talking this mess. You're like a disobedient child! How many times do I have to tell you about this love shit? Love got your ass broke, and disgusted both of y'all for that matter. We don't fall in love. Not in this clique! Love makes you vulnerable and a liability! Can you see, Jay, or are your eyes blind to what's going on out here? How many people in love do you see that are actually happy? A nigga can spot a dumb bitch a mile away and that's why they do the shit that they do!" *Why do I feel like I'm always repeating myself talking to Jay? She doesn't get it.*

"Hold up La, you going a little too hard now. None of us are dumb. We might not make the best choices, but it happens. I'm just looking at it like this, if Jay wants to find her soul mate that's not a bad thing. Just because you or I don't believe in soul mates, don't knock her." *Now Binky wants to play both sides. She's so understanding, when just a minute ago she was ready to jump in Jay's ass.* Binky can be a little two-faced at times, just depends on which one of us she's with.

"Shut the hell up, Binky! Exactly how much have you two bitches had to drink? Both of y'all are drinking stupid! No more Ciroc! Next time, we're going brown! I got this suite to cheer you two up because lately y'all been down in the dumps. I surely didn't get it for y'all to blow my buzz with this nonsense! We're supposed to be in here turning the fuck up. Instead, I feel like I'm at a funeral. Shit, I could have saved my money! I need my chicks on point, no new stuff! The motto stays the same, 'GET THAT MONEY!'" La said angrily.

CHAPTER 2

LALA

I was standing in my condo admiring my view overlooking the water. It was so peaceful. Growing up on the east side of Baltimore, in the projects, really made me appreciate this type of living. I vowed to get out and make a come up for myself. And I did exactly that...no matter the cost.

Working wasn't something I was willing to do after watching my mother work day and night, only to still be struggling. Daddy played the in and out game. He would pop up every now and then to see to my brothers and me, but that was about it. My father never took us anywhere or really spent any quality time with us. Even when he showed up, it was never about us. It was just to gas Mom's head up again, for her to give in, and for him to disappear until the next time he got a little itch. He wasn't shit, which caused a strain on my relationship with my mother. I really didn't have any respect for her as a woman. Why be bothered with a man if you're still going to struggle and he can't help?

I never understood women like my mother, and I made a promise to myself to never be her. Women need to understand that gold mine that sits in-between their legs. That's why I taught my girls, Valencia a.k.a Binky and Jaylin a.k.a. Jay, 'If you ain't getting nothing but a wet ass, keep your legs closed.' He has got to pay.

My circle was small and that's the way I liked it. You can't roll with me if you don't look the part. You can't call yourself 'high maintenance' looking like shit on a stick. That wasn't going to cut it. The body had to be banging and the face had to be beautiful. If you didn't have the whole package then you weren't hanging with me, nor would you ever be a part of my clique.

Me and my girls are all of that...and then some. I do get the most attention; I'm that brownie that you never get enough of looking at. I mean really, what more can a man ask for when he's getting my five-five, brown skin, hazel eyes that I was born with; hips, a round ass, thirty-six D-cup and my weave is always on point. I wouldn't even look right hanging with an average chick. It just wouldn't be fair to her to have every nigga drooling over me, and never her.

*****

Tiz and I were going real strong until Swift came into the picture. Tiz was making pretty good money promoting and taking care of me, but I wanted more. Let's just say, greed at its best. We had a nice apartment and I always had money in my pocket. He wasn't great in bed, but that wasn't even a factor. The almighty dollar moved and soothed me. I don't even care what you look like, just keep me out the ghetto and we good.

Some say I'm a gold-digger, but I call it keeping the pussy paid. I'm not walking around here broke, my needs and wants are met to the fullest. So when Swift approached me, and his money was much longer than Tiz's, I went with the man that had the most to offer me. I didn't mean to hurt Tiz, but truth be told, I could care less about anybody and their feelings. I had to play the role and act like I cared because every time I turned around Swift was getting caught up with some little has-been. But until I catch a bitch in my condo, and my money starts slowing down, then and only then, will he catch hell. No matter who I'm with, you will respect me. See, being with Tiz, I never had these problems. If he was out there messing around, shit never came back to me. The only bitch that I have a problem with is Diamond. For some reason she just stalks the hell out of me. She ain't nothing but a trap queen who doesn't mind having my hand-me-downs. That's the one thing I'm not doing; getting my hands dirty. Jail ain't meant for me, in no way, shape or form. He can go to jail if he wants; I bet I won't be there, on to the next I go. I'm not your 'hold you down' type of chick either.

There were others before Tiz and Swift, but I had to bounce. If your ass ain't out in thirty days, time's up my man...and trust me, by day fifteen, I'm already plotting on the next one to take care of me.

These bills roll in every month, faithfully, so I need my money like clockwork.

That's the difference between Binky, Jay, and me. See, they get their feelings all caught up…that's why they're back in them projects. When Juice and Stone got caught up, there went their money. They were out here paying for lawyers and making every court date like they had it like that. I tried to tell them, 'think smart, take the money and keep it for yourselves.' In other words, a rainy day would come, and sure enough…it did. Both of them were left broke with nothing. The feds came and took everything; houses, cars…froze their bank accounts and the whole nine-yards. They didn't have anything in their name. *Stupid, stupid, stupid.* My condo and my car are in my name, even though Swift paid for everything. I had to be smart because too many of these chicks are left with nothing. Even in my worst-case scenario, if I had to sell this condo and downgrade to something else, I could. For now I will just keep banking my money. To top it off, I had investments in my dead grandmother's name, just in case the feds tried to seize my shit. I will always be able to get to a dollar. Securing me was everything, because like I said, I'm not working for no one. It's not even a thought.

Every now and then, Jay would get to talking stupid about getting a job. *A woman shouldn't be working.* Who wants to work and only come home with four to five hundred dollars a week? *My piss is worth more than that.* What in the hell can I do with that? I can't even buy me a *Michael Kors* pocketbook, not to mention, my

Dolce and Gabanna jeans cost me twelve hundred a pair. When I walk out the house, I'm wearing at the very least, two G's on my body. I'm accustomed to a certain lifestyle and I need to be kept up at all times.

CHAPTER 3

JAY

I was getting myself together to go and walk over to Binky's.

Bink only lived one building over, so it wasn't far at all. Being back in these projects for the last six-months was six-months too long. This was so degrading…going backwards from riches to rags. Plus, the two of us were the hot topic for a long minute. It's no fun being a part of the laughing stock. Me and Bink had to figure out something.

Two minds together were always better than one, especially when we both needed a come up. The roaches and mice were on a serious take over in these projects, and once you got out, it was hard as hell coming back to this lifestyle. Not that I forgot where I came from, but I damn sure didn't see myself ever coming back to this. I have to shake everything out before I even get dressed. I tried bombing the place, but the more I bombed, the more the roaches came. The other day I set up ten mousetraps and within fifteen minutes all ten traps were full to capacity. Every day it was the same old nasty shit.

Complaining to Jock everyday wasn't getting me anywhere. All he ever said was, 'Baby it will be okay.' *That's cause he ain't living in this hell-hole.* On any given night somebody was always shooting. The beef was strong in the projects. You had to be careful or else you would catch a stray one. Lala keeps saying be patient...that one of these days, Jock is going to surprise me. *Yeah well, when? I'm tired of crying myself to sleep at night. I'm not as strong as I appear.* My only escape is when he takes me to the hotel. I cry every time we have to leave, and lately he's been getting them short stays, or he tries to get some in the car. *I can't keep doing this with him. I miss Juice so much.*

The part that's killing me is Jock knows how I was living. If he wasn't going to be able to keep me at my standards, then why even bother? I'm just ready to be regular. Get a job and have my own funds.

Every now and then I made some extra change by doing make-up. They call me the beat master. I can make an ugly chick look good. *I should go and apply at Mac and see if they will hire me. I would love to do something like that.*

Lala's philosophy doesn't work for everybody. I know she's gonna be pissed, but she's sleeping good at night. I even asked her if I could stay over at her place for a couple of days, but she came up with every excuse in the book. She blamed it on Swift having a fit, but he wasn't like that. He would be glad that I was there. That would give him more time to handle his business; half the time he ain't home anyway. She wasn't fooling anybody; she just didn't want me there.

Bink was handling her living situation. She was the most hood out of us three anyway. You could put her in a desert and she would find a way to make it alright.

I even tried to get my grandmother to move. She's old enough to move in a senior building, but she won't do it. She likes living here. The other night she was up talking to the mouse. I'm an only child. My mother passed away when I was three. I vaguely remember her. No one likes to talk about how she died so I don't pry. I'll let that be their little secret. My father got shot out here, in these same projects, when I was six-months old. So, all I ever had was my grandmother. She did the best that she could do, no complaints over here. Living on a fixed income, trying to take care of a child can't be easy.

That's why I don't want any children until I can provide some stability. I look around at all these young girls having these babies by these no good ass-men and it disgusts me. It's like, what are they thinking? Do they want to be just another one his baby mamas? Didn't you know that he didn't work before you had the child? Why make life twice as hard as it already is? Lala always gets on me for thinking too much, but that's just me. I have to think things through. She claims that I'm the softy out the bunch because I care too much.

I'm okay with caring. I can't be like her, just because a nigga gives me money, I'm supposed to be okay with that? I want it all; I can't be with you if the sex is whack. You have to tickle my fancy; I enjoy being and feeling loved. What Juice and I had was special and I want that kind of love with somebody. He's doing a twenty-year bid with no parole. The last letter that I received from him was telling me to go on with my life. Only a real man would ever tell a woman that. I just recently stopped visiting him because it was too hard on him every time he saw me. *Enough of thinking, let me go over to Binks and see what she's doing.*

*****

"Gram, I'm gone. See ya later." I walked out the door. As I was walking towards Binks' building I saw Binky sitting on the bench wiping away what seemed to be tears. I went and sat down next to her.

"Hey Bink, what's the matter with you?" I wasn't used to seeing Binky in such a vulnerable state of mind. And she was out in the open; we hide our troubles on the inside.

"Hey Jay. I'm okay. Just having one of those mornings." Binky gave Jay a slight glance.

"You want to talk about it? I was on my way over to your place." Jay said.

"Jay, have you ever wondered what life would be like if we had our mothers?" Binky looked at me with bloodshot red eyes. "Sometimes it gets to me. All I ever had was my uncle. No mother, no father, no cousins, not a grandmother to call on or an aunt. The list goes on like I have no family. I feel so alone at times."

"Don't say you don't have any family because you have me and Lala. Sometimes family ain't what it's all cut out to be. La has her whole family and she doesn't visit them or anything. They are so estranged you would think that she's just like us. But I do feel you. Every time my mind drifts towards my mom, I block it out. I just can't let myself go there too often. You know how they say you can't miss what you never had; well it's not the truth. You end up wanting it even more; it's a yearning on the inside that you can't even explain. I just always imagine my mother being nasty, mean, and at her worst. Because I never got to know her, it helps me cope a lot."

"You do that?" Binky smiled shaking her head at me. "Girl, you are crazy but I can see how that works. Gives you a sense of 'I'm better off.' I have to try that. I just always picture my mom being the opposite. In my mind she's this woman that's just full of love. Whenever I ask Uncle about her he just clams up and gets mad at me. I told him I want the truth about my family…that I need to know. Whatever it is I can handle it. I'm a grown woman now! He went in his room and slammed the door shut. I got nothing!"

"Wow! Well you know my Grams is very closed-mouthed when it comes to my mom. I just feel like when the time is right for her, she will tell me the story. I see her sometimes just pulling out the pictures of my mother with tears pouring out her eyes. Sometimes I just try and comfort her, other times I just let her be.

After all these years, I figure whatever it is, my Grams is trying to spare my feelings and protect me."

"I'm sorry, Jay. I disagree. We are not kids anymore. What gives them the right to hold information from us, whether good or bad? What could be worse than what we already been through? I keep watching these shows on TV; you know the ones where the adopted kids or parents are trying to find one another. Something in me is missing. I don't feel complete and I'm always angry on the inside." Binky was pouring her heart out.

My eyes filled with tears because I found myself in the same state of mind that Binky was in time after time. I know the pain that she's feeling. That's why I just had to find a way to block it from her mind. "Binky, you just have to replace that emptiness somehow, so that way you will feel full."

"I've been doing that all my life. That's why I'm always ready to fight at the drop of a dime. I feel so good once I release all that frustration but it only lasts for a little while."

I noticed the neighbors were setting up nosey shop, looking out the windows and sending out their eye spies to walk by fifty times. "Bink, let's just go to my place, we can continue our conversation there. We don't need to give these people any more gossip to go on. You know that we will be on the project news faster than we can get into the house."

"You're right," Binky laughed. "Let's go!"

CHAPTER 4

BOSS-MAN PLAN

"Listen up ladies! I got word that Boss-man is going to be at Secrets tonight. So we are going to Anne Arundel County. Tiz is getting us in and we are going to be in the VIP section." Lala said with excitement. "We have to be on point. I want us all to look flawless for him and his crew. If one of us can land him, then we're going all the way to the bank. Remember, if one gets on we all get on. So how much money are we working with?"

"Girl, the other night I watched Moose count up twenty-five G's and he only put five hundred in my hands. What the fuck I look like, stupid? I'm so tired of this penny-pinching bullshit! Then I had to give my uncle two hundred of that for his rent. I'm only working with three, and that ain't nothing. I don't know how flawless you want us to be, but I do have that dress that I wore at Nay's party. I can put that on." Binky said.

"Binky, calm down. I know how you feel though. Jock only gave me two out of his fifteen." Jay smirked.

"Two what? G's, I hope!" Binky looked at Jay like she had five heads.

"Nope, two hundred, and I spent twenty five of that. I'm not messing with these cheap hustlers' out here on these streets no more. We need a come up, for real! We need real money. By the time I pay my grandmother her rent and pay my cell bill, I'm broke!" Jay shook her head in disgust.

"Well, give me what you have. We need outfits for tonight. Bink, we need hair and not that cheap stuff either. See if you can call in a favor or two. Jay, I need you on you're A-game tonight. Beat the hell out of these faces. I want Boss-man to ask for us, not us asking for him. One of us should be able to land him." Lala said with much confidence.

"Hold up, what do you mean one of us? What's going on with you and Swift? And does he know where we are going tonight? You don't need to be messing up! Tiz is enemy territory and Swift takes care of you very well! He put you in a nice Condo, you drive around in a Benz, plus he keeps them pockets fat! You need to stay in the background. Let me or Jay get on." Binky said and Jay nodded in agreement.

"I hear you Bink, but let's not get it twisted. Swift does pretty well out here in these streets, but Boss-man is the hottest producer out here on the planet right now. He's getting millions, not thousands. Not to mention it's legit money. I would be a fool…plus Swift is messing with Diamond and he's trying to play me for a fool. The way I see it, may the best woman win." Lala threw her hands up in the air.

"I'm just saying Boss-man is not guaranteed. We might just be another one of his groupies. What makes you think he's messing with Diamond? She can be dealt with. My name is Binky and I'm known for cutting a bitch up!"

"Binky, didn't that judge tell you he doesn't want to see you no more in his courtroom? You need to stay out of this! I'm not trying to visit my girlfriend behind bars. You're on probation, you get in trouble you're looking at five-years, plus whatever the charge is! Don't talk stupid!" Jay said very irritated, rolling her eyes.

"Jay is right, Bink. I can handle Diamond when the time comes, but right now we got this little business to handle. I need to get to the mall and find us some dresses and shoes to wear. Less is going to be more. Boss-man likes his chicks raunchy; we are showing all the curves and cleavage tonight." Lala stood up and walked around in a circle. "POW! WOW! We got ass for days ladies, and we didn't buy it…we were born like this. Ain't no way he's turning all three of us down! One of us can land him. Now, while I'm gone I want you two to do some studying. Look him up. Find out what his likes and dislikes are. What he's into…we need to know all of that. Just so when he comes at one of us we will know how to converse with the man. Are we good?"

Jay and Bink both nodded their heads in agreement as Lala walked out, headed to the mall.

*****

"I hope she knows what she's doing! If Swift finds out that she's still keeping in touch with Tiz, all hell is gonna break loose. She's going to find herself by herself!" Binky said shaking her head.

"I know, I was thinking the same thing. We've been down this road before with Lala and her great ideas, and the two of us ended up losing out. It was like The Great Depression, remember? Back home in these projects that I hate so much, shit ain't been the same since. We need our own money, not hers." Jay walked over to the window to see what all the commotion was about, and of course, the kids were out there in the parking lot fighting again. "Every day it's the same thing over and over again."

"We're gonna come up again, we just have to be patient. But I know one thing...Moose and Jock have got to go. They are not holding us down like they should and could be doing. We still in these projects...we don't have no whips and we always broke! One of us needs to land Boss-man or somebody in his entourage."

Jay hated to admit it, but Binky was right. "Binky, you need to get us that hair. You have to do both of us, plus your own. You could be getting started on mine now."

"Shoot, I almost forgot. Let me text Lexi now and see what she says." Binky sent the text out asking for some hair on credit. Shouldn't be a problem, Lexi knew she was good for it. Sure enough, Lexi said to give her thirty-minutes and she would be here. "She's on her way. Let me get you washed and dried so I can start braiding your hair."

"Okay." Jay followed Binky to the sink. "I'm getting nervous about tonight, like in a good kind of way. This just might be the break-through that we need."

"Yes, let's hope so. May the best woman win, just like Lala said…and really it don't matter because all three of us look out for one another. Girl, your hair is dirty! I just washed it two weeks ago."

"You know my hair holds dirt, but you're wrong about looking out for each other. Let me correct you…me and you look out for each other. Lala is selfish. She just took our last when she knows she gets money. We don't have it like her. She should have said, 'I got y'all!'" Jay was starting to get in her feelings. "When I was on I didn't ask y'all for shit! I treated all the time."

"Yeah I peeped that a while ago, but don't you worry I got a plan. Lala ain't gonna have a chance at Boss-man because she's not going to be there. We are!" Binky turned the water off and grabbed a towel.

"How we gonna do that when she has to bring us there?" Jay asked looking puzzled.

"Oh, she's gonna bring us. We need them dresses and shoes. I plan on letting Lexi know a thing or two. Trust me, she will tell Diamond and best believe Diamond will tell Swift. That's all we need. Everything else will fall into place." Binky was certain her plan would work.

CHAPTER 5

DIAMOND

I was waiting for Swift to pick me up so I could go get my new whip. I custom ordered a black CLK, identical to Lala's. I was only doing it out of spite. *We might as well drive around like twins since we are sharing the same man once again.*

Lala was always my rival when it came down to the men department. I'm tired of coming in second place all the time. *If Swift wants to be with me then it was gonna be my way.* I have no intentions on creeping with him in the near future. I want all of him, not just a piece. I heard his horn beeping and ran outside. *I'm excited about picking up my car.*

*****

"Hey!" I gave him a peck on the lips as I hopped in his car.

"Hey! You look nice. Smelling all good. Where you going?" Swift pulled off.

"Thank you. I wanted to be looking the part since I'm going to be driving the part. I can't be in a Benz looking half-ass." I purposely put on my cut up jeans that hugged my hips and ass nicely, with a pair of my six inch red bottom, rainbow shoes, my red half shirt, leaving my stomach out, and my diamond necklace and earrings…to match my name. I slid closer to Swift, gazing in his eyes.

"You know what you're doing! You are not slick, trying to blow up my spot! As soon as Lala gets wind of this, she's going to have a fit! That's what you want, ain't it?" Swift was two steps ahead. By this time tomorrow, Lala was getting an upgrade. He was picking up her Bentley. That's the only reason why he agreed on getting her an identical Benz.

"Well, I just figure if she's good enough for one then I am too." Diamond moved away and sat back.

"Come on Diamond, the same exact one? They make all kinds of Mercedes and you just had to have that one. You loved that Infiniti but wouldn't get it because you so busy trying to prove a point. You have to remember that you ain't my girl. I just fuck with you. Don't get me wrong, I like how we vibe. The chemistry is there, but my home is elsewhere."

"I'm tired of hearing that. I know who you belong to, but I also know where you be and it ain't with her. Every time I turn around you sniffing up my ass. She can't be getting any kind of time! She thinks you out here getting that money and handling business, but most of the time you're with me! She has no idea how you operate your business. I'm the one putting my life on the line for you! Where is she at?" Swift had struck my nerves.

"Yo! You always get angry when I tell you the truth. You knew what you were getting into from the jump. I told you...always been honest with you. I'm not playing no games. I love Lala. She's been riding with me for a minute now. If I knew you were gonna get attached I would have never touched you!"

"So let me ask you this, can I get a man? I mean, I'm single, and I will just see you on the side! I think that will work better for me." I could see the anger in Swift's eyes.

"Naw! Not if I'm taking care of you. He damn sure ain't driving around in some shit I paid for. Now, if you find one that's willing to take the bill and pay me for the car, then we can talk. You won't be pimping two of us. I'm not having that."

"Wait a minute! Everything that you give me, I earned it. Dealing with you is like having a job. You come and go as you please. You stash your product in my apartment. Your boys come in and out as they damn well please. You conduct all your business transactions there. Whenever you feel like digging in my pussy and ass, you do! When you're hungry, no matter what the hour, I get up and fix you something to eat! If the cops come running up in my shit, I'm going to jail, right along with the rest of y'all! So what is it that you think you're giving me? If you really sit back and think,

I'm underpaid!" Now I was giving Swift the truth and from the look on his face, he wasn't liking it.

"You chose all of this. Now you want to come at me? I had a stash house but you said 'No, come over here' because you wanted to spend time with me. You welcomed my boys! You told me you didn't want me eating out…that you would cook for me! You knew the risks you were taking, now you putting it all on me! This is what I'm going to do for you!" Swift picked up his phone and called Moose.

*****

"What up man? It's a beautiful day in the neighborhood." Moose was talking in code letting Swift know that everything was good on his end.

"Good, good. Listen, I need for you to make a move. Remember them pies that I like at Shop Rite? I need for you to go and get them, put them in a brand new refrigerator for me. The ones I have left are hot! I can't eat them anymore. I'm afraid they might make me sick!" Swift's way of telling Moose to move his product

Moose, getting the message, replied, "Alright main man, I'm on it right now. Hopefully I can have that done by tonight before they close. Let me see if I can get me a babysitter so I can take care of that for you. I will holla later!"

*****

"You didn't have to do that! Your product is safe with me." *I forgot how immature Swift could be at times.*

"Oh no, you only get once to throw some shit up in my face. All activities are shut down from your apartment." Swift pulled into the car dealership. "I'll wait here for you to get the keys, just to make sure everything goes okay."

*****

I jumped out of the car, pissed off, and walked into the dealership to sign the rest of the papers and get my car keys. *I can't believe Swift was trying to play me like this.* While I was waiting for them to pull the car around, my home girl, Lexi, called with some pertinent information. *I'm gonna use this to my advantage.* My CLK pulled up, looking beautiful as ever. I walked outside to observe and make sure it was everything that I wanted it to be. After doing a thorough inspection, I walked up to the driver's side of Swift's car for him to roll down the window. He had his music on blast...bopping to the music.

"Is everything straight?" Swift asked turning down the music.

"Yes, seems to be. I'll know more when I pull off." I shrugged my shoulders. "So, will I see you later?"

Did this chick really just ask me that? "Naw! I'm busy this weekend, maybe one day next week. I will see. You know I have some moves to make."

"This is what it's coming down to between us? I thought we were better than this. She can go hang out with Tiz and Boss-man tonight at Secrets but I can't have you!" I started walking away. Swift jumped out the car running up to me like a mad man.

"What did you just say?" Swift had to ask because maybe he was hearing things.

"You heard me! Lexi called and said she gave them some hair on credit. The three stooges are going out and her ex is promoting the event. I told you she wasn't loyal to you! Why don't you take a ride and go out there and see for yourself, because if you call or let on that you know she won't go. I'm just coming from a woman's perspective." I jumped in my Benz and pulled off laughing. *That's what he gets.*

CHAPTER 6

SECRETS NIGHT CLUB

$\mathcal{L}$ala, and Binky were sitting side-by-side looking in the mirror at how well Jay beat their faces. All of them were pretty, but makeup just enhanced their beauty to a different level. Kind of like, put them in a different category from all the other girls. It was time to put on the dresses and shoes that Lala got from the mall. All three complimented their figures lovely, but Lala's stood out the most. Not because she had the better shape but her selfishness set in when she was at the mall. Binky looked at Jay and they both nodded.

"What seems to be the problem, ladies?" Lala asked noticing some disapproval.

"You said less is more. All I have is this split and shoulder hanging off. The dress is nice, but I thought it would be more revealing." Binky said while she was still admiring herself.

"I had to work with the money you two gave me. All our dresses are Versace and you know how much they cost. I did the best I could. Plus, we all look flawless and that's all that matters. These fringes on this dress are starting to get on my nerves." Lala was getting agitated. "They keep flying all over the place. I'm trying to be sexy not slutty."

"You're right, we didn't have enough money. Our men don't hit us off like Swift does you, but we're good. I'm happy being Plain Jane. My three little splits will be enough! When you try too hard, you lose. I think being kind of conservative will work for me." Jay wasn't worried about the dress because even if the plan went south and Lala got in, Boss-man wasn't looking for her type. After reading several of his interviews he likes a woman with class and this dress was doing it for her.

"I can't help it if Swift takes care of me. It's not my fault that you two let them men of yours throw pennies your way." Lala said while still trying to get them fringes under control.

"You right," Binky just smiled knowing she had plans for Lala's ass. "I can't argue that point. That's why I'm going out here to find someone better."

"Okay ladies, let's roll!" Lala strutted to her Benz with Binky and Jay following behind her.

The ladies didn't talk much the whole ride there. They were all just anxious to find out what the outcome would be. They arrived at nine, right on time. The line was around the corner. Good thing they had VIP access and wouldn't have to wait to get in.

*****

"Well come on ladies! What y'all standing around for?" Lala asked staring at them.

Binky and Jay were hoping to see Swift out here somewhere but they didn't. Giving each other the eye, they just followed suit. Tiz let them in and escorted them to the VIP booth. Boss-man wasn't in the building yet so the ladies got comfortable. Sitting on the couch and drinking some drinks, suddenly, out of nowhere came Swift. Binky nudged Jay.

"Look who's here," she whispered in Jay's ear.

"Oh shoot! It's going to be on and popping up in here!" Jay said.

Swift went up in the booth grabbed Lala's hand and walked her all the way out of the club. Lala was playing it cool. The last thing she needed was a scene, plus he had a hell of a grip on her hand. Swift opened up his car door so he and Lala could get in.

Grabbing her by her neck, he said, "What the fuck is up with this shit? You must think I'm playing with you! I told you to cut all ties with that nigga, but you out here trying to play me!"

"Swift, get off my neck." Lala removed his hands from her neck. "I'm not trying to play you; you're trying to play me. Yeah, I saw you earlier at the car dealership with that bitch Diamond; she drove off in a car just like mine. Damn right I called in a favor from Tiz! You're never home, always in these streets, probably with her, and I'm always in the house waiting on you. Those days are over."

Lala was pissed. *He has some nerve coming at me when he's the one cheating on me.*

"Me and Diamond ain't like that. There is nothing going on. I was stashing my product at her house, so of course I have to be around her. It's business, and yes, I told her I would get her a car as payment for the use of her house. All you had to do was ask me...not jump the gun." Swift said, sounding sincere. "You over here calling your ex for favors when you know I can't stand old dude with his corny ass!"

"You know I can't stand her. Diamond and I have history! I want your product out of her house and now! Every man I've ever had...somehow, some way, she ends up in the middle! I'm not driving around in the same car as her either! You can call me when that's done. Until then, just stay away!" Lala went to open the car door and go back in the club. Time was ticking.

"Hell no! You are not going back in there with that on! You look like a slut! Everybody doesn't need to see my goods. This is not a video shoot...it's a club! Now I will take you home to change and then bring you back here. Look at this," he said, pulling up her fringes and seeing her bare breast. Swift started up the car, drove to the back where nobody could see, laid Lala's seat down and started sucking on her breast.

"Swift, not now! I want to go in the club and have some fun with my friends."

He didn't listen. Next thing she knew he was up in her for what seemed like hours. She wanted him to be done already. Lala had one thing on her mind and that was Boss-man. Finally, he finished.

"I changed my mind; we're going home so I can hit it the way I want to. This car ain't doing it for me." Swift had been dealing with Diamond so much he forgot how good Lala's pussy was. He had a strong appetite for her tonight, and she wasn't going anywhere.

"I drove the girls here, how are they supposed to get home?" Lala asked.

"Give me your keys. Never mind, I have mine! They can drive themselves home tonight! I'll be right back!"

Lala couldn't believe Swift. She couldn't wait to ask him how he knew where she was in the first place. She put this whole thing together and didn't stand a chance. Lost in her thoughts, she heard the gunshots go off. *POW! POW! POWPOW! POW!*

CHAPTER 7

JAY

*I*n two weeks time I was living the life. Boss-man and his entourage had just come out to party with the crowd. DJ Goon was doing the most. The music was popping, so Binky and me started rocking to the music in our VIP booth with our drinks in-hand trying to play it cool. I could see Boss-man staring at me from the side of my eyes, so I put an extra sway and step in my groove. I saw him point at me and nudge his bodyguard. To no surprise the bodyguard walked up to me and said, "My man would like to meet you." I was playing a little hard-to-get so I took a chance and said, "I don't know who your man is. If he wants me then a gentleman always approaches a woman." *Lala taught me that move long time ago.* "It's Boss-man; ain't nobody got time for you to be playing games! You coming or not?" I replied, "You heard what I said." Truly, I wanted to run over there like no tomorrow, but I gambled with this one and it paid off. By this time Binky was looking at me in disbelief. It worked out in my favor; Boss-man had his bodyguards escort him over to me, and he introduced himself.

"Hello," he said with his hand extended out. "I'm Teddy Graham, but I'm known as Boss-man...the reason why you're here."

"Hello, I'm Jay nice to meet you." I smiled. "I came with my friend; she wanted to come here tonight because you were going to be here."

That's all that was needed before the gunshots rang out. Boss-man grabbed me and had me smuggled up between him and his bodyguards. They led us to the back of the club where his custom made Lincoln Navigator was and he scooped me up and put me in it. The driver pulled off. All I could think was, *Where is Binky?* Once things settled down in the truck, I called her three times, back to back, and got no answer. Then panic-mode set in. I wasn't leaving Binky in no cross fire, even though I knew she had the keys to Lala's Benz. Friends just don't do friends any kind of way.

"Wait, I have to go back! I can't leave my friend!"

"You see that car behind us?" Boss-man asked.

I turned around and looked at the car that was following us but I wasn't sure what that had to do with getting back to Binky. "Yes, I see it."

"She's in there. You didn't strike me as the type to leave a friend behind. Calm your nerves, I made sure that she's okay." Boss-man looked at me as if he could eat me right then and there.

"Oh, thank you so much!" I was very much relieved.

Once I knew that Bink was okay, it was party time. We went back to the hotel that Boss-man was staying at. He rented out the whole fifth floor. It was nice because all the adjoining doors were open, so we went from room to room partying our asses off, having a ball. That night was epic.

Somewhere around four in the morning Binky came and found me and Boss-man. We were just sitting around chilling and talking. Binky was tore up from the floor up, hollering 'can somebody bring me back to my Benz?' Not only was it not her car, but I'll be dammed if she was driving. Period.

Boss-man was such a gentleman. He followed me, with Binky by my side, staggering to find her an empty room to sleep in. I found one at the end of the hall and I told her to go lie down in the bed. She laid down and went fast asleep. Boss and I sat down in the two chairs by the door.

"Why don't you come to my room? Your friend seems to be sleeping well." Boss asked.

"No, I'm not leaving her in here by herself. There are a lot of people roaming these halls and opening up doors. I'm going to sit right here until it's time for check out." I didn't trust that Binky would be alright. I already got a glimpse of what was going on in the other rooms. Groupies everywhere, and I lost count of the disrespectful bitches that were trying to get ahold of Boss-man in my face. These people were drunk and high and nothing was going to happen to Binky on my watch.

"Well I guess I will sit right here with you." Boss-man said, not wanting to be out of my sight. "You can lay on me if you want, I'll watch you sleep."

I did exactly that. Fell right to sleep in Boss-man's lap. I was exhausted and this was much better than going home to the roaches and mice. I slept until ten in the morning. I remember Boss-man saying that they were checking out at eleven. Bink was still in the bed, snoring.

"You slept good and you talk in your sleep." Boss-man said looking down at me.

"What did I say?" *I hope that I wasn't talking about the wrong thing.*

"Don't worry, it was all good." Boss-man laughed at me. "Listen, you need to wake up your friend. It's almost time to check out. I was wondering if you would come with me? I'm on this little tour promoting some of my artists. We're going to a couple different states."

"Sure, I'll go with you." I was ecstatic. I tried playing it off, but I knew that I answered too quickly, without hesitation. If he could only feel how I was feeling on the inside. "I will have to go and get some clothes."

"No, I'll just buy you some. I'm glad you're coming. Thought you might have turned me down. You have been giving me a hard way to go. A man like me isn't used to this type of treatment. Most women would have left their friend and been in the bed with me."

"Yeah, wrong chick." I laughed. *The hustle was starting to work.*

"Nope, right chick…for me anyway. Listen, I'll go round up my people so we can roll out of here by eleven. By the time I do that you two should be ready." Boss-man lifted me up so he could stand up.

"Binky's coming with us?" I had to be sure. I didn't want any miscommunication.

"Yes, if she wants to. That way when I'm doing some running around you will have some company."

"You're going to buy her some clothes too?" I asked.

"No, I'm going to let her stay funky and nasty. Of course! She's with you so she gets treated too. Now get her ass up so we can roll if she's rolling." Boss-man was confident that Binky was coming. He knew her type quite well.

*****

We were gone for two whole weeks. Lala was having a fit sending us all kinds of text messages. Asking where we were. Texting she needed her keys back. So Boss-man had the keys shipped to her overnight. That was so funny to me and Binky. She was trying to hold some keys over our heads.

The only regret that we had was not being able to attend Tiz's funeral. The night them gun shots went off, he was shot and killed. I have a really good guess as to who killed him. He was a good dude; Lala shouldn't have been entertaining him like that.

Outta all the places we went to, I really enjoyed myself in Miami. I could easily move out there, with no problem. Bink and I had the time of our lives. Traveling, shopping, eating good, drinking, meeting all kinds of celebrities, taking pictures…and Boss-man, not only did he make sure my pockets were fat, but he also made sure Bink was straight too. I wasn't trying to spend all mines. I was watching what I spent my money on because I knew that I had to go back home. I needed some money to carry me through. I had to put that buzz in Binks' ear so that she would have the same mindset as me.

Somebody let Jock and Moose know that we went on tour with Boss-man because we were both getting cussed out by them. Do you think we cared? Hell no! We weren't passing up an opportunity of a lifetime for some niggas that wasn't even taking care of us. Lala had to tell Swift in order for it to get back to them.

On our last day in Miami, Boss-man flew us home. He said he enjoyed spending time with me and was looking forward to the next time. I wanted to cry my heart out. Bink wasn't happy either, but we both knew that this day would come. It just went by too fast. Yep, time flies when you're having fun. Home Hell Home, because it wasn't sweet.

*****

"Now what are we going to do? Just go back to these projects and deal with them two sorry asses." Binky was angry from the moment we got to the airport to go home.

"I don't know about you, but I'm not going back today. We have money and there is a hotel up the street. I'm checking in to figure some things out. This life right here ain't working for me. I'm happy for the moment, and I want to stay that way, even if it's just for a minute. I'm not rushing back to depression." I was adamant about that. I called Grams every day and night that I was gone to check in and make sure everything was fine.

"Well I'm following you. We can go half. I'm not trying to see that place either. Let's just catch a cab up the street." Binky was relieved. The longer we stayed away…the better.

CHAPTER 8

LALA

I still wasn't really feeling Swift after he shot and killed Tiz for no reason. To top it off, Binky and Jay going on tour with Boss-man really pissed me off. *My blood is boiling. That was supposed to be my opportunity.* Swift was home a lot lately. One, because he was trying to prove to me that him and Diamond wasn't an item. Two, because he was laying low. The cops were asking a lot of questions. I would have turned him in had I been with Boss-man; then I wouldn't need his money. This Bentley he bought me was a nice gesture and I did look good cruising the streets in it, but this did not excuse the fact that he took a man's life.

Now is the perfect time to ask him about taking me on a trip since he's kissing ass. Swift has never taken me on a vacation. He's always so busy or afraid things are going to mess up if he's gone too long. *I don't want to hear about my girls being here and there. I need to have one to top all that shit off, and a vacation will do it. They'll be back trying to flaunt it in my face when I'm the one that planned the whole thing and spent money buying those dresses.*

That's exactly why when Swift asked me where they were because Jock and Moose was looking for them, I spilled the beans. I wasn't covering for them. And then they had the nerve to Fed-Ex my keys. They just left my car at the club. All I got was a text from Binky telling me to go get my car, that they were straight. Then when I told them that Tiz passed away, you would think that they would have come home to at least make the funeral. Nope, they were too busy having fun and didn't even check on me.

Their broke asses will need me before I need them. They're the ones back in them projects. I'm still sitting my pretty, smart ass in my condo that I own. They don't know that I'll trade them in for two smart bitches. Bitches that know how to work their magic on these niggas and get paid. They better get some act right in them and quick because I will be on the hunt for some sure nuff female hustlers.

"What you over here thinking about? I hope it ain't that bitch ass ex of yours! He ain't coming back so you might as well get used to it." Swift said with an attitude. "You always looking down at the water like you want to be floating in it."

I turned around and looked at Swift as if he had lost his mind. *I hope he wasn't threatening me. Bitches won't be the only thing I'll be on the hunt for if he keeps up this nonsense.* "I picked this place because of the view. You know that. You threatening me doesn't scare me. It only makes me re-evaluate this relationship."

"Oh really? Well you should re-evaluate yourself. I'm not going anywhere and neither are you. I put too much money into all of this." Swift pointed at Lala waving his finger up and down. "Walking away from me would be your worst mistake."

"Where's Diamond? I'm sure she's pretty pissed off that you've been over here with me and not her. Are you two having problems?" I laughed trying to be funny. *He has got to be kidding me. I can't walk away, but he can fuck my arch-enemy? He killed a man that I only called for a favor. Good and crazy is what he is.*

"I told you, wasn't anything going on. I moved my product so now I don't have to be over there as much." Swift tried to hug Lala from the side but she moved away.

"Really Swift? Miss me with the bullshit. Your reason for being gone all the time was because you had to keep an eye out on your product. Just because you moved the product from her place, now you don't have to keep an eye out? Yeah you moved the product and your dick too. Don't play me for no fool!" I was waiting for the next lie that Swift was going to tell.

"How many times do we have to have the same conversation? I'm tired of repeating myself over and over again." Swift grabbed his coat.

"Actually, I like asking you the same question over and over. If I were the police you would have been locked down. The first time I asked you, you said she was holding the product and you were paying her for her good deeds. The second time I asked you, you said she was trying to mess with one of your boys and that's why she was always around. The third time I asked you, you said she was holding your product and trying to get with you but you always turned her down. The fourth time I asked you, you said she was holding your product but she had connections that you needed. So from all of that, I know that she had your product. But your shit doesn't add up! Come again, Swift-baby! How many more turds you got in ya?" I was finding Swift amusing.

Swift started putting his coat on. I had just pissed Swift the fuck off. I was beating him at his own lies.

"See, this is what I don't have time for. This nagging! You want to come at me, but let me explain to you that I need a dime on my arm, a Diamond in the bed, a sweetie pie's chef in the kitchen, a Florence from the Jefferson's, and a ride or die. Sugar, at the moment you're only fulfilling one. A dime you are, but I kept you that way...an upgrade from the corny dude. You're living this lifestyle because of me. I pay for that hair on your head. I pay for that Bentley that you drive. I pay for the maid to come in here and clean up after your messy ass. I pay for the food that you order out! Technically, you're a broke bitch with a pretty face and a fat ass! Without me, you ain't nothing. Understand that! You ain't bringing nothing to the table but a damn bill! So go sit your ass down somewhere and wait on me to come home!" He slammed the door and walked out.

"Oh yeah?" I was walking around the condo swinging my scarf. "This bitch thinks he can do me any kind of way! By the time I'm done with you, you're going to be licking my toenails one by one, motherfucker! Oh I'm gonna get you if it's the last thing that I do! Nigga a setup is on the way little do you know it! As soon as I get my shit in order, your ass is going all the way down! The Feds is gonna be my best friend! I'm shutting the whole operation down including Diamond. That bitch is gonna get hers one way or the other. A closed mouth doesn't get fed and I need to eat right now. I'm very hungry!" *I would go to my girls with this but at this point they can't be trusted. I'm rolling solo on this one here. No problem, I got this!*

CHAPTER 9

JAY

I had just got off the phone with Boss-man. He said that he missed me and wanted to fly me out to L.A.. Of course I said yes. He said I could bring Binky along with me again. Another trip for us at his expense. *Binky was gonna be one happy camper.* We still hadn't been back to the projects. We had been in the hotel for a week now, splitting the cost. Nor had we contacted Lala and she didn't reach out to us either, which was fine by us.

*****

"Bink," *I hate when she has them headphones in and can't hear shit.* I walked over and took them off her head. "Girl, I got something to tell you."

"Oh, okay, what's up?" Bink sat up on the bed. "You're all smiles so this must be good."

"Where did me, you, and Lala always say we wanted to go?" I asked.

"No, say it ain't so! We're going to L.A.?" Binky jumped up as I nodded my head. "When are we going?"

"Tomorrow morning. Boss-man is paying for our plane tickets. He said that I could bring you with me again. I can really get use to this life." I wasn't sure where this relationship was going but I was feeling high off of life right about now.

"Yes. What about Lala? You think we should call and tell her? We can brag on this shit."

"No, we are not calling her. She doesn't even know that we're back. I'm still getting nasty ass text messages from Jock. If we call her she's going to run her mouth and then we will have to deal with Moose and Jock. I'm not up for all of that. We will call her when we get there. She broke all the rules when she ratted us out. She won't be happy for us anyway." I knew that Lala was going to be pissed the hell off once she found out that we were in L.A.; a place that the three of us had always dreamed of going.

"You're right, but that's so stupid. She has her own money; she could have come with us. She's missing out." Binky just shook her head.

"Yeah, that's what happens when you hate on the next bitch. Her problem, not ours. Let's get packed up because we are the hell out of here first thing in the morning." No way was I, or Bink going to entertain La and her foolishness. She wasn't gonna mess with our flow.

Binky and me stayed up half the night talking and laughing. Morning wasn't coming quick enough for us. We couldn't wait to get on that plane. We weren't sure how long this trip would be this time, but any time away from the hood was good time, as far as we were concerned.

CHAPTER 10

MOOSE & JOCK

"*M*an, fuck them bitches," Moose said to Jock. "Why the hell do you keep texting her?"

"Man, she's not even responding to me. She act like she ain't never got to come back here and face me." Jock said.

"Who cares? You over there ego-tripping, Tracey is getting ready to have your baby any day now. This is an easy out for you. Nigga you better take it and run. I know it's not something you planned, but you caught up now." *Jock got some nerve. I know my shit ain't right, that's why I stopped trying to call and text Binky. I'm over it, let her do her; I ain't even mad at her.*

"Yeah man, Tracey was just a side thang. She trapped me. I really wanted to help Jay out, but then this bitch goes ahead and gets pregnant. She's staying in an apartment that was meant for Jay and me…not me and her. Tracey ain't even my cup of tea. She was just something to do at the time." Jock was looking around making sure his workers were on point.

"Well you should have thought about that. Strap the hell up! You always run up in pussy raw. Now that shit just cost you a lifetime. It ain't a bitch out here getting me caught up unless that's what I want. Right now all I want is the almighty dollar. That's my high. Binky was singing that same old tune. I don't know who she thought I was or who she thought she was. I could have been nice and put her in one of my properties that she doesn't know anything about, but then I would be losing money. Money is my first bitch. That's who I love…everything else is secondary. They might get a couple of hundred out of me but that's it." Moose was so serious. Wasn't a pussy out here that could run him or have him all in his feelings.

"Man you foul as shit. Money come and money go. You say that now, until your ass gets old and lonely." Jock laughed.

"I won't be old and lonely. Not as long as I have a dollar. These trifling women out here will dive at fifty cents, show them a dollar and they think they hit the jackpot. All I have to do is spoon feed them. I'm not looking to be claimed no time soon. A bitch can think what she wants, but ain't no stakes over here." Moose said grabbing his cock.

"Alright man," Jock realized this conversation was a lost cause. "What are we going to do about this situation with Swift?"

"He's out of control. That's my man and all, but he be doing some stupid ass shit. I can't roll with him on this. He should have checked his woman. Now he got our situation hot, putting all of us in jeopardy. He laying low but got us out here on Front Street. This ain't cool at all." Moose shook his head.

"I was thinking the same thing. We're already watching over our shoulders. Dude was loved by many; he was a good guy just trying to make a living in the right way. I heard that the funeral was out the door. You already know that somebody saw him do it. I mean at least wait until the club closes or something. We just have to keep our ears and eyes wide open." Jock was in disbelief that Swift could be so reckless knowing the life that they live.

"What I'm getting ready to say has to stay between you and me, it goes no further than the two of us and this car. You got it?" Moose waited until Jock shook his head in agreement. "I hope that whoever saw Swift shoot old dude, that they come forth before we feel the wrath. At least if he goes down then we can breathe a little. This shit right here has hurt a whole community. You should have seen all the people on the news. We can't win this war by ourselves. We have to get off these streets."

"So, what are you saying?" Jock asked.

"I'm saying that it's time to promote. Pick two of your guys that you trust to do what we do." Moose waved his finger around at the five guys on the block.

"I can do that easily, but Swift is going to have a fit." Jock took off his hat to scratch his head. *Now this going to cause trouble.*

"Don't you worry about Swift because his pretty ass ain't worried about us. Once we get our guys in place, that's when we tell him. If he ain't gonna be out here playing eye-spy day and night, then whatever he says holds no weight. We need to be laying low too. We're a part of his clique, which makes us an option to die. Are you willing to risk your life for a murder that you didn't commit? It's one thing if we did it, then we have to be man enough to accept whatever consequences that come our way, but I'm not going in the ground for some unnecessary bullshit."

"You right." Jock had to agree. Swift was the one that made a bad decision not them.

"Hell yeah, I know I'm right. Just think about that baby you got on the way. Do you want your child growing up without you behind another nigga? Swift ain't as loyal as you think he is. If he was, then he would have told us what I'm telling you. What makes him think that his life is more important than ours?" Moose had a made up mind. He had already promoted his two guys. He was just doing Jock a favor by putting him down.

"Okay I'm about to pull up my two tonight. Fill them in on the ins and outs; see what they say. But, I'm almost positive they will bite." Jock was sure that his men would jump at the chance.

"Alrighty then, I'll holla." Moose jumped out Jocks car and then jumped in his.

CHAPTER 11

SWIFT

"You have been over here a lot lately. What's wrong, trouble on the home front?" Diamond laughed. *Shit was funny to me. I tried to tell him. I knew he would be back sniffing up my ass.*

"I'm just chilling; don't worry about my home life. That's none of your concern." Swift grabbed the remote to change the channel on the TV. "I'm hungry, can you fix me something to eat?"

"No, you can go home for that; I'm going to stay in my place. That's her job. She needs to make sure that her man eats." *He gets no more of that. Swift got it messed up with me.*

"Fine! I'll order out. You ain't said nothing but a word. I got money so I can always eat. How about you? My product ain't in this apartment no more, so how you think you're going to get paid?" *She wants to be a smartass then I'm going to be even smarter.*

"I'm good, Boo. See, that's your problem…always thinking that somebody depending on you. I was taking care of myself before you and I can take care of Diamond after you. I'm not that ho that you live with. She needs you…I don't."

"Can I take my car back now? Or do you plan on making them payments?" Swift asked. *She acts like she got this all under control. I'm calling her bluff.*

"You can take that car back. I'll get another one. She's riding around in a Bentley, you should have got that for me! She doesn't deserve that shit! What does she do for you? When your birthday came around, I gave you a gift. I buy you stuff just because. Has she ever put you before herself or does she always have her hand out? Yeah, that's what I thought. You nice and quiet over there with nothing to say. Please tell me what that bitch has on me? She don't do half the shit I do, but yet y'all niggas always running behind her."

*****

Swift jumped up and grabbed his coat to get the hell away from Diamond before he knocked the shit out of her. *She was really trying to push it. I know she heard about me killing dude. I can't trust myself. Right now I'm on edge; anybody could catch it. It's time for me to catch up with my boys anyway.* I drove over to both spots and there's no Moose or Jock. *Now I have to find out what's going on with this.*

*****

"Yo,Yo, Yo," Moose answered.

"Man, where the hell you at?" Swift asked.

"I'm chilling in the house. Trying out this Play station 4 I just copped." Moose could hear it in Swifts voice. *He must have drove around to the spot.*

"Where is Jock?" Swift asked.

"He's probably at his crib chilling. I talked to him earlier."

"So y'all not handling business these days? We work around the clock. Let me know what's up!" Swift said with an attitude.

"We have everything being take care of, it just ain't by us. You laying low and so are we. I'm not getting killed because niggas got a hit out there on you. We chilling just like you been doing." Moose was waiting for Swift to come back at him.

"It ain't even that serious. I'm laying low because of the cops, not no niggas. I'm good. They know better than to come for me. I'm the last person they want to have a problem with. Y'all acting all scared and shit." Swift wasn't trying hear it.

"We ain't scared, we just ain't trying to die before our time. You made things hot around the way for us. We're not trying to deal with none of it! I'm still trying to figure out what you were thinking. Shit was stupid!" Moose said sounding very aggravated.

"Look I had already warned him once to stay away then he went and disobeyed my orders. I had to make an example out of him." Swift didn't understand why Moose was acting like he didn't know him. It wasn't like it was the first time he had to go to extreme measures.

"Naw man, we handle business when it comes down to these streets. Fuck these bitches! If you leave today or tomorrow Lala is going to be fucking with the next big thing. That's just how she rolls and you already knew this. Dude was not a threat to you…his money wasn't long enough. You act like she got you wide open." Moose replied.

"Man I'm not wide open, it's a respect thing." Swift said.

"Respect thing? Remember how you got her? You took her from him and you talking about respect. You and Jock are stupid when it comes down to pussy. The same way you get them is the same way you lose them. That man wasn't bothering you or her. If anything she disrespected you." Moose wished Swift could hear just how dumb he sounded.

"Forget all of this, I need for you and Jock to be looking out for this money. I told you before; you can't trust these dudes. Now you putting me in a situation where I might have to handle somebody else." Swift said.

"Look man, I'm gonna tell you like this. If you so worried about that money then you put yourself in a shoot-em-up zone. Since you're the only one that's not worried about nothing. I'm not doing it and neither is Jock!" As much as Moose loved money he wanted to be able to live and enjoy it. *He must think we stupid. Let him be naïve by himself since he thinks he's so untouchable.* Moose hung up the phone.

Swift was sitting in the car thinking to himself. *I'm getting real tired of these clowns and bitches that are trying to check me today.*

I'm not putting up with too much more of this. I'll take them all out. Does Moose know who he just hung up on? He thinks he can call the shots now? Does Lala know that I'm about two seconds away from whooping her ass? Does Diamond realize who I really am?

CHAPTER 12

JAY

*B*inky and me arrived in L.A.. As promised, Boss-man had a car there waiting for us and the driver took us straight to the hotel. Boss-man had some work to do so he wouldn't be able to see me until later, which was fine by me. That way Bink and I could get some sightseeing done. Once we checked into the hotel we bounced right back outside.

The weather was gorgeous and we weren't too far from the strip, so we decided to walk and see what we could. It was still morning here so breakfast sounded like a good idea. Both of us were hungry. We stopped in this place called *Canele*. It looked to be very upscale. We were hoping we could afford it but once we were seated and took a look at the menu, prices weren't too bad. Binky ordered some waffles with bacon and I got the chicken and waffles.

It didn't take long for the food to be done either. We thought we would have to wait a while because it was so crowded.

"Jay, do you really like Boss-man or do you just like him for the money?" Binky asked.

"I really do like him," I was a little puzzled by Binks question, but I guess I can understand why she would ask. "Why you ask me that?"

"Because you know how we are. We have dealt with plenty just because of that dollar. I didn't know if that was the case this time or not?" Binky took a sip on her orange juice.

"He's a nice guy I could really get into, but I'm scared. I'm not trying to get hurt and with him being him, I know he has plenty of women all over. I'm not sure where I fit in at." I was feeling uneasy from just the thought of losing Boss-man to the next chick.

"Well you need to find out where you fit in. Just ask. I'm kind of feeling someone myself, but he doesn't have a lot of money. He's a regular kind of dude. Jay, I just want to try someone different. I'm tired of the same old same." Binky said.

"Wow, who is it? I had no idea. You've been holding back on me. I thought you were just hanging with me for the ride." *Binky is crushing on somebody in Boss-mans crew.*

"Well you know how it is in our clique. We're supposed to go after the dough. I wasn't sure how you'd feel about it. We've been hustling our whole lives. Using our beauty and bodies to get what we want. We still don't have anything. The guys we chose to mess with did. I want some things for myself...things that nobody can take from me because I got it on my own. This shit is overrated. You know what I'm saying?" Binky looked like she wanted to cry. Her emotions were starting to get the best of her.

"Awww Bink," I reached over the table and put my hand on Binky's shoulder. "It's okay, I'm not going to judge you. I've been feeling the same way ever since we had to go back to where we came from. I'm tired of chasing a dollar. If he's somebody that you want to be with, then go for it. I'm not going to judge you."

"I feel so much better now that I got that off my chest. He doesn't even know that I'm interested. I've been just watching how he moves and the way he carries himself. So far I like what I see. We speak here and there...just a simple hello. Please don't tell Lala, she will have a fit and make me feel stupid."

"I'm not telling her anything and remember she's not our mother. She doesn't control us. Since we're getting stuff off our chest...I've been thinking a lot about La, and I'm really not feeling her. I love her because we've been rolling so long but when I go back and look at things she's one trifling bitch. She has always treated us like her flunky's. Her hustler game ain't all of that. She's just in a better situation now than she ever was. She throws it up in our face every chance she gets. She wouldn't even take us in and she has three bedrooms. She watched us cry our asses off when we lost everything and her only come back was 'step your game up, ladies.' What happened to helping us out?"

"She did help us...by hooking us up with two cheap asses. That's her kind of help. We of all people know how she is. She's out for herself. I was locked up because she had beef with bitches and she didn't bail me out. You did! I got a long list of the shit that Lala did to me. She will get her day! The well will run dry and she will watch us shine!"

"Speaking of shine, I'm going to call her and tell her to fly out here. The three of us need to talk because I'm tired of holding all of this in. What do you think Bink?"

"I think that Swift is not letting her go anywhere. You know how he is, but you can try."

"If she does come, my main priority is still going to be Boss-man. He sent for us and I'm not kicking him to the curb for her. She wouldn't do it for me." *If La does show up she's going to be expecting me to be running up her ass, not happening.*

CHAPTER 13

LALA

*T*he best thing that could have happened to me was Jay making that phone call. They're down there in L.A. having a ball without me. Hell yeah, I flew on the next thing smoking. I only packed a small bag, a couple pairs of panties, bras, perfumes and deodorant. Swift was pissed. I texted him when I got on the plane.

By the time I got off the plane seemed like he had text me a thousand times. My phone kept going off for about thirty minutes straight. Little did he know I would no longer need his services. I got my own plans. My first mission is to have Boss-man to myself. *Jay thinks she can just steal my man. I can show her better than I can tell her.* Those two all booed up every five minutes and in my face like I'm supposed to just eat that shit. Binky and her stupid ass running after the hype man like I ain't peep her drooling over him.

We don't fuck with the help; we go after ballers and ballers only. *She better get it together. I taught her better than that. I'll do this shit with them tonight but tomorrow I'm up and out early, leaving both of them behind.*

I overheard Boss tell Jay that he had some business to take care of; he has some new talent that he's scouting out. All I have to do is find out where, and best believe I'm taking my pretty ass right where he's going to be. I've been trying to get him to myself, but Jay is always in the way. *Bitch, disappear already.* She ain't about this life. I taught Jay and Bink how to hustle pussy. I'm a master at it, and trust me, Lala gets what the fuck she wants. Bitches better get behind me because that's where they belong. *All these random dudes in my face, please step away, I'm not interested. Look at Jay over there laying by the pool with Boss putting lotion on her. Makes me sick. Now here goes stupid walking up to me.*

*****

"Girl why are you over here by yourself? Reese is trying to holla at you, he's about to go on tour. Girl, he's going to blow up." Bink wanted to know why La was over here all standoffish like she was stuck up or something.

"Is he selling out arenas?" I answered in my snotty tone.

"No, but he will be once he gets on." Binky answered sounding all excited like it was a big thing.

"Girl please, do you know how long that might take? If I wanted Swift money then I would have stayed my ass home with him. I'm out here to come up. Unlike you, your hustler game is getting weaker and weaker. You must like being back in them projects." I tried to shew Binky off. She was blocking my view from keeping a close eye on Boss.

"La, you came down here on some other shit. What about just having fun? Oh, I forgot you don't know how to do that anymore. You're too busy still trying to be an overpaid prostitute." *Did Binky just try and play me?*

"Watch your mouth, Bink. You been doing a lot of traveling that your probation officer don't know nothing about. Be very careful how you try and handle me." I rolled my eyes.

"You really want to try me? Because I do have Swift's number and the same place he put Tiz, is where you can go too. So fuck with me if you want!" Binky was talking to me as if I was a bitch off the street that she would do in at any given moment.

"Hey, what's going on? What's all the noise about? I heard y'all from way over there." *Here comes dumb ass Jay running up to us to save the day. I'm glad we made enough noise for her to get up and let her pussy breathe.*

"Nothing. She can't take a joke. Bink, you know that I would never do that to you."

"No I don't either; ,'t even crack a smile. You were dead ass serious." Bink was standing her ground.

Jay was looking back and forth at the both of us while Bink and I had our eyes locked on each other. If looks could kill, we would both be dead. I should have just kept my cool with Bink, but I'm not letting no slouch talk to me any kind of way.

"She threatened to call my probation officer and tell her that I've been out of town without permission like I don't have time over my head. La has been very salty towards us since she got here." *Here Binky goes telling on me like Jay is going to do something.*

"La, you didn't say that to her! Please tell me that you didn't go there!" Jay walked away looking like she was disgusted with me. *Yeah, I said it!*

*****

Boss-man jumped up like a puppy in training hugging on Jay like the weak bitch that she was. See, I could handle my own; he wouldn't have to be bothered with no nonsense. I would have handled the situation. He glanced over at me so I put on my sexy pose like, 'Come to me daddy, come get you a real woman.' I know he sees me in this two-piece that I have on just for him. I saw him glancing in another direction when I turned to look and see what had him so engaged. It looked like Binky was leaving the pool party. *Good I'm glad, now I don't have to worry about her for a while. I see Boss-man is finally getting away from Miss Thang. It's a perfect opportunity to follow him and make my move. He walked in the bathroom but I think I'll give him a few seconds before I go in behind him.*

"Hey Boss!" All his business was hanging out. *Not too bad down there either.* I guess I caught him off guard, he wasn't expecting me. He kind of tried to jump and turn his business to the side, but too late, I had already seen enough.

"Do you always walk in the men's bathroom? I'm trying to use it if you don't mind." He sounded like he had a bit of an attitude, but I'll fix that.

"Not really, but you're a hard person to catch alone. I came all this way just to see you. I'm the prize that you need in your life." I got up close and personal while he was washing his hands. *It's good to know that he's clean.*

"What if I tell you that I'm not interested? I've already been given the perfect gift." *Evidently Jay has the man brainwashed.*

"Then I would have to call you a fool. You could give me a trial run just to see if I can prove you wrong." I pulled on his shirt.

He had the nerve to remove my beautiful hand. "I thought you were a good friend of Jay's, was I mistaken?"

"We are good friends, but I was the one that you were supposed to meet that night, not her, and she knew that. The way I see it, she took something that didn't belong to her in the first place."

Boss-man bent down to whisper something in my ear. *It's about time for him to see things my way.* "Even if you were there, I would have still picked her. From the way that you carry yourself that lets me know that I made the right choice. I need a woman of substance and you don't have that attribute. It's such a shame. All that beauty with missing components isn't going to get you anywhere. You need a couple of classes from Jay so she can show you how it's done."

"Classes from slow boat, are you fucking serious right now? You must need to be re-schooled, in the industry that you work in. You need a ten, not a nine and a half. If I'm on your arm, I can help you blow this industry up."

"You need to come down from whatever high that you're on, sweetie. I have a twenty on my arm and you're about a five. If you keep your mouth closed then you're about an eight."

"Fuck you, asshole!" The next thing I know Boss-man was having me escorted out of the hotel. *It's all good. We will meet again and he will eat every word that he said to me.*

CHAPTER 14

SWIFT

I called Diamond over here to the condo to give her some good news, but this chick keeps talking about she don't want to come because Lala lives here. I told her bring that ass and now. Of course she came once I used a little bit of force.

"Swift what did you call me over here for?" Diamond was speaking in the buzzer. I ignored her and buzzed her in. She got off the elevator running her mouth. "I'm not up for no drama, Swift! Your bimbo lives here, so what is this about?"

"You been watching too much of that Springer show. This is not a set-up, girl. Come in and sit your ass down." I motioned for her to have a seat on the couch.

"Alright but that bitch better not be in here." She sat down like I asked her to.

Diamond was looking around. "I have to give it to her, this is pretty nice up in here. I underestimated the bitch. I thought she was only certified to dress and be a label ho but it looks like she has a little more talent than lying on her ass."

I had to laugh at Diamond, when it comes to La she's always saying something slick out her mouth. "Naw she didn't do this, we hired an interior decorator."

*****

"I knew it was too good to be true. I can't even give her that credit then."

"Enough of her, I want you to move in here with me. I've been doing some thinking and I want you." I sat next to Diamond and grabbed her face. "No more sneaking around, let's just make this official."

"Excuse me?" *Is this Swift really talking to me?* "Why all of a sudden? Just a couple of days ago you stormed out. What happened to all that stuff you were just saying to me?" Diamond called herself trying to be funny by throwing shit back up in my face.

"I told you that I'd been doing some thinking and you made me realize some things. She never bought me shit. She's a problem that I have to solve. I can't do this with her. You're right, you deserve all of this." I said looking around at the condo that I'd been paying for.

"Oh now you want to see things my way. I been telling y…"

I kissed Diamond on the mouth to shut her up. "That's the past; I don't want to discuss it anymore. I'm giving you her Bentley too, just like you said."

"What?" Diamond smiled as if she had just hit the lottery. "Wait a minute! Isn't that in her name? She's always bragging about everything being in her name."

"Diamond, here you go again. I have everything taken care of. I know people in high places, anything that I need done gets done." I walked over to the kitchen table and threw Diamond a set of keys. "The big key is the one that lets you in the door downstairs, the other one lets you in here, and the one that's not really a key works for the Bentley."

"Where is she? Did you kill her?" Diamond was starting to ask me too many questions.

"No, I didn't kill her. I sent her on vacation so I could set stuff up for you to move in." At least that's what I wanted Diamond to think. *Since Lala wants to play with me, she needs to be dealt with in a special way. I'm sending her back where she came from, which was nowhere.* "You're special to me, Diamond, so why should you have to sit back in the cut when you belong front and center?"

"Aww Swift, you did all of this for me? You just made me the happiest woman breathing."

"Well I'm glad. You deserve the best and I'm going to give it to you. The sky is the limit; I'll move mountains for you if I have to."

"Where the hell is this Swift coming from? I've never seen him before!" Diamond sat on my lap. *Could this be the man that I've been dreaming about all my life? This right here feels so damn good.* "I know I don't say it often, but I love you Swift."

It's funny how Diamond can tell me that she loves me and Lala never does. The more I'm sitting here talking to Diamond the more I realize that I'm making the right decision. La don't love me, she loves my money. If the cops ran up in here right now I could depend on Diamond to do some real gangsta shit. La, naw, she would be worried about her damn self.

"You are that ride or die Diamond. I know that I can count on you to have my back."

"I kept trying to tell you that she has never had your best interest. I've seen her and her crew work these niggas for years now and bleed them dry. My ass is bigger than hers, but you don't ever have to worry about me selling it or selling you out! I felt sorry for them dudes. I could never figure out how they couldn't see right through her. Her pussy must be on some platinum shit to have niggas mesmerized. Not only was it the men but she has Jay and Binky under her spell too. They don't know that after all these years, that bitch will be the one to get you killed and walk right by your dead ass bodies and spit! She's a ruthless, trifling ho. I'd rather go head-to-head with the devil himself, than to roll with that snake ass bitch."

"Okay, Okay, I don't want to spend the rest of the night talking about her. All I want to do is concentrate on you and me. That situation is dead and buried." I picked up Diamond and carried her into the master bedroom and laid her on the bed.

"Oh no!" Diamond jumped up. "The first thing we need is a new mattress and box spring. I will not be sleeping on nothing that she slept on." Diamond opened up the closet and saw Lala's clothes still in there. "These have got to go also; anything of hers needs to be gone before I move up in here."

"Okay, I will have the maid remove all of her things as soon as she gets here in the morning." Diamond was making this transition much harder than it had to be. I'm a man of my word so whatever she wants, she gets.

"Maid? You mean the bitch don't clean either? Baby, listen, after tomorrow you can fire the maid. I know how to clean and you already know I'm doing the cooking. We can save that money! Why, oh why, was she here? What good was she?"

"I'm not firing the maid. She's an old Italian lady; Ms. Isabella, and I like her. She needs her money just like the rest of us." *I changed my mind; Diamond could have ALMOST whatever she wanted because my maid ain't going nowhere.*

"Well okay, I forgot you do have a heart sometimes." Diamond laughed. I didn't find that funny. *Of course I have a heart.*

"Plus, you're going to be busy anyway; I need you to help me with this business. With me, Moose, and Jock laying low these days you're the only one that I trust to oversee some things. The cops are not gonna be looking in your direction. All you have to do is scope things out, make sure everything is going smoothly. If it's not, then just make that phone call."

"I got you, Boo. I know what you need. But back to this place and that Bentley. Now that I have keys should I be worried about her coming up in here?" Sometimes Diamond doesn't hear me too well. La ain't getting up in here.

"I had the locks changed; she can't get in, and I had the key to the Bentley reconfigured. You're straight." I assured Diamond once again; hopefully it would be the last time. "I'm going to have Isabella get rid of all her stuff and I don't care what she does with it. She can give it to the Goodwill or keep it for herself if she likes."

"I finally got this bitch after all these years. I can't wait until she comes banging on that door. I'm gonna laugh my ass off just like she used to do to me. I always told her that I would have the last laugh. Now where's she gonna go with nothing." *Here Diamond goes with the Lala rant again. Didn't I say that I don't want to waste no more time talking about her?*

"I have another surprise for you." I lifted up my shirt so Diamond could see my new tattoo.

Diamond screamed loud enough that every neighbor on this floor could hear her. "I can't believe you got my name tattooed on you! Oh, I really have to watch my back. Swift, I'm so happy. I love you so much baby! Can't believe I doubted you!" Diamond grabbed my hand and walked me into the spare bedroom. "Oh it's on and popping, poppy!"

CHAPTER 15

LALA

I was running around the airport screaming, "Where the fuck is my car? I can't believe y'all let somebody steal my shit!"

"Miss, please calm down, your car wasn't stolen. A young gentleman came and picked it up the other day." The stupid valet supervisor was responding to me.

"You just let some dude come in here and take my damn Bentley? I'm going to sue the hell out y'all! Watch, watch!" I was walking around in a circle with my finger swinging in every direction.

"He had a key, Miss. People leave their cars here all the time and their loved ones come and pick it up while they're gone. If he didn't have a key then he wouldn't have been able to drive it out of here." The valet supervisor and the rest of the crew were just standing there looking at me as if I was the crazy one.

"I'm leaving, but I'll be back!" I said feeling real stupid. *Swift must have come here and picked up my car. Now I'm calling him back to back and he won't answer. I have no other choice but to catch a cab home. But the question is, how did Swift even know where the car was? Because when I texted him I said I needed time away. So now Binky wants to play with me, but I'm the type of toy that you never touch.* I paid the cab driver, got out with my luggage and headed upstairs to my condo, but my key isn't working and neither is my access code. So now I'm ringing the bell like crazy and texting this motherfucker at the same damn time.

*****

"Who is it?" *I know damn well that this ain't Diamond's voice on the intercom.* "Yes, can I help you?"

"Who the fuck is this? Let me the fuck in and now!"

"Oh honey, you no longer reside here. Swift didn't tell you that he had all your stuff removed? I'm sorry for this mishap, he should have told you or at least gave you some kind of warning."

"Bitch, where is Swift?" *I know damn well Swift don't have this bitch up in my shit. Who does he think he's playing with?*

"He's sleeping like a baby. Every time I ride the hell out of that dick he falls asleep. Did you have that same problem?"

"Diamond, all I see right now is your blood on my hands! Bitch, I'm going to fuck you up something terrible. By the time I'm done beating your ass your own mama won't recognize you! Are you sure you want to play with me?"

"Oh my God, I'm so scared right now. Are you threatening me?"

"I don't make threats; I do make promises that I'm known for keeping! Why don't you come down here for a minute?" *This side bitch has overstepped her boundaries.*

"Where are you going to stay? If I were you I would check into one of the homeless shelters and see if they have a room for a homeless bitch like yourself!"

"First off, the deed to the condo that you have your raggedy infested ass in, is mine. It belongs to me, so I'm going to count to ten before I call the fucking police and have both of y'all escorted out of my shit! Then I will catch you sometime this week bitch, to deliver my promise to you!"

"Actually you signed the deed over to me, you don't remember? Stay off that shit La, it's doing something to your brain!"

CHAPTER 16

JAY

I was lying around in the room waiting on Boss-man to finish his work for the day. I had been feeling down for the last couple of days, trying to replay in my head when everything went left between Lala and me. Being here without Binky wasn't making it any better. Bink left the day that Lala threatened to call her probation officer. I tried to convince her that La was only bluffing but she wasn't taking any chances. I made sure that Boss-man wasn't looking when I slipped her the five G's that he gave me. I wanted to make sure that she would be alright until I got back.

I'm not sure what La ended up doing...don't really care either. Out of all the years we've been hanging, certain lines we never crossed. We've been glued to each other since middle school and not one of us ever tried to holla at any man that was even remotely connected to the other. If dude even tried to holla and even if nothing did happen, he was automatically untouchable. That's just how we rolled. Over the past month, Lala had crossed many lines that I just let go. She was my girl. We did a lot of dirt together. You would think that you get better with age. Not her, the worst was consuming her.

We're all twenty-five now; time to settle it down a few notches. I know eventually I want a family. Right now I'm still having fun, but when I settle down, I'm not going to be running out here in these streets. Growing up we all had it hard. Our families didn't have any money to buy us what we wanted. If we were lucky we would get the bootleg version, but all the kids would laugh at us, so authentic it was. That's why we started out boosting to keep up with the rest. Then when the stores caught on to us we started getting arrested, but we were all minors so in the juvenile courts nothing really stuck. We would have had to do something really bad to get put away. We knew the system so we didn't care. All we did was move on to the next mall or put on a disguise.

The older we got the more attention we received from the guys. Lala said there was no need to boost when you look as good as us. She said we could prey on the boys and it worked out. Lala led, and Binky and I followed. At first we weren't giving up anything, but after a while you have to put out or get shut out. One by one we were getting cut off from the money. By the age of fourteen we had become pros at the sex game. Oral came a little later. Lala had us watching porn so that we could learn how to suck a mean one. It wasn't long before we all caught on. The point was to get whomever pussy whipped and once you accomplished, that dude will move mountains.

Protection didn't play a role until after we started catching them STD's and Binky got pregnant. Lala had two fits yelling at Binky, 'What the hell you gonna do with a baby? You messing up our clique. I can't hang with no chick and her baby.' She acted like having a baby was a disease instead of being a gift from God. Once Lala put all that stuff in Binky's head, next thing you know we all headed to the abortion clinic. Binky said it was the worst experience of her life. Binky didn't even know who the father was so we just kept it quiet. One of plenty secrets that we kept to ourselves. If Binky would have had that baby I would have stood right there by her side.

*****

"Hey you!" Boss-man walked into the room bending over to give me a peck on the lips. "Have you been in here all day?"

"Yes, just thinking. I just felt like laying around." I had no energy, mentally I was drained.

"Sweetheart, you've been like this for a couple of days now. You have to snap out of it." Boss sat down on the bed next to me. "Life is hard. She won't be the only snake you run into. You just have to handle the situation."

"I know, it's just hard. We've been through a lot together. She always talked about keeping our little clique together, sisters for life." I was in my feelings and couldn't control my tears from streaming down my face.

"I don't like seeing you like this." Boss-man reached over and grabbed some tissue from the nightstand to wipe my tears off my face. "What can I do to make you feel better?"

"I don't know. I will be okay, eventually. When I have to go back things just won't be the same." I slid myself up on the bed.

"Who says that you have to go back? What if I want you to stay here with me?" *Was Boss-man asking what I thought he was asking me? Now that's a sure enough way to dry up these tears.*

"How am I going to stay with you when you're always on the road? What about your other female friends?" I wanted to know what Boss-man's intentions were before I made any lifelong commitments.

"I want to settle down here in L.A. for a while. I'm going to rent a house out. I'll...or should I say, we, will be here for at least six months, if not longer. L.A. has some amazing talent that I want to establish. I just signed two people. I'm going to be in the studio, but that doesn't mean you can't come. And as far as other women, you don't have to worry about that. My eyes are lit on you."

"This all sounds good; I would love to stay here with you. But let's face it, I don't have anything to offer you. I need a life of my own; a job with steady income. I'm tired of depending on men to take care of me. Before Binky left we were having this same discussion."

"Sweetheart, you were dealing with the wrong type of men. I see something in you that you don't even see in yourself. I don't mind taking care of you, and I'm not trying to brag, but I do have lots of money. How I'm gonna pay a bill is never an issue with me." Boss-man laughed. "I do understand you wanting your independence. If you want to work I can get you a job. Just tell what you want to do and I will make it happen for you."

"I love making women feel beautiful. I'm good at doing make-up. Are you going to be faithful to me? I see how this industry gets down. I don't want a man that's going to be out here cheating and stuff." *I'm scared as hell to give my heart to him and then have him make me look like a fool.*

"Why didn't you tell me that you like doing make-up? I can plug you in; you could have been doing the make-up for some of these video shoots that I've been doing. And to answer your other question…one woman at a time for me. I haven't been in a relationship in a while, but I think that we can make it work."

"I hope so. I need to call my Grandmother and Binky and let them know that I'm not coming back anytime soon. I know they will be happy for me."

"Are you happy for you?" Boss-man questioned me. "I'm sure you're gonna want to go back and visit from time to time."

"Yes, I'm very happy. It's just that every time I get comfortable, something bad happens. I have so many emotions running through me right now and I'm scared to fail." *Now I'm sounding really vulnerable, I shouldn't have let that slip out.*

"I can tell. Your body is shivering. Can you manage to get yourself together? I have a nice, quiet evening planned for just the two of us. We're always around a bunch of people; I want to show you something a little different."

"Well you are the Boss. I guess I can do that." I would do anything for him, plus I needed something to take me out of my funk.

"Good, I'll be back at eight, be ready." Boss-man kissed me and walked out the door.

*****

I'm calling Bink right now. "Hey Bink, what's going on up there?"

"Nothing, same old same. I finally came home today, back to this rat hole. I was staying at the hotel but had to think about stretching this money. Of course these fools around here couldn't wait to tell me that Swift threw Lala out, moved Diamond in and gave her the Bentley."

"Oh shit! What the hell? Damn, damn, damn! Where's she at now?" *I'm surprised somebody finally left La.*

"Who knows, probably laid up with the next. You know these people are so nosey these days. I just kept my cool. Then Moose stopped by a little while ago and gave me the 411. I think he was fishing for information on where she's at. When I told him what she said to me in L.A., he was pissed off. He said 'let the bitch rot!'"

"How did he even find out that you were back? Never mind, stupid question. I know where we live at." I rolled my eyes. I knew the moment Bink stepped back in that courtyard Moose's phone was blowing up.

"You already know, so what's going in L.A.? If you see Freddy tell him I said hello. That last day I was there was the first time I actually had a real conversation with him. He wanted to take me out to dinner that night but I hopped on that plane without even saying goodbye."

"Freddy, oh okay I got you now." *Now I know who Bink is crushing on.* He was the MC that opened up for most of Boss-man shows. I would have never put that one together. Freddy wasn't Binks type at all, little short brown skinned dude with crooked teeth. Bink always liked her men tall, big, and dark. "I was calling to tell you that Boss wants me to stay here with him. He's going to rent us a house. Anytime you want to come and spend some time with me I will send for you. Just don't tell anyone that you're going out of town."

"I figured that you weren't coming back. I'm happy for you, but sad at the same damn time. As soon as you two get settled I'm the hell out of here. Boss is gonna get tired of seeing me." Binky laughed. "Hey sis, at least one of us made it out. I have an interview on Monday at Shefty's. If I get it, I'll be a sales associate. It's better than nothing."

"That's great! Well, at least its high end clothes. I'm sure you will get some good money in commission working there." I felt my mood changing. Talking to Binky was lifting my spirits. "Listen I have to go but don't forget to check on my grandmother for me. I'll tell Freddy what you said, plus add a few things of my own. Love ya girl!" I hung up the phone and jumped in the shower to get ready for my date.

CHAPTER 17

LALA

I walked into the Federal Bureau of Investigations and signed in on the sign-in sheet. The lady at the front desk said it shouldn't be too much of a wait. *Good, because I'm ready to get this done and over with. I'm shutting down Swift's whole operation.*

I called the police and tried to prove that the condo was mine but the deed was inside the condo. I called the mortgage company to get a copy, only to find out that Diamond was right, my name was forged and signed over to her. Then when I tried to get my stuff the cops said that I have to take Swift to court because he wasn't letting me in. I tried to have the gas, electric and cable shut off, but none of that was in my name anymore. I went to the Department of Motor Vehicles to get the title to my car, and that too had been signed over without my permission. There was nothing they could do either, unless I could prove it somehow.

Whoever signed the title did a good job because the signatures matched. Then I go to the bank…all the money that was in the joint account was gone. I couldn't use any of my credit cards. I was fucked. *Swift did me in, now it's time to do him in.* Now I had no other choice but to dip into my stash. How the fuck you gonna move the enemy into my home, give her my car and all my belongings. I don't even want the shit anymore.

I've been looking for Diamond, but I can't seem to catch her, but I did catch the car parked outside her Aunt's house one night. I smeared my bloody pad all on the window to what used to be my Bentley. Now normally I swear by a tampon, but this was a special occasion that only a pad would do. Good thing I was flowing heavy and had plenty of blood clots to push out. Then I spray painted 'I'M COMING FOR YOU BITCH!'

I'm staying with my mother for now while I'm looking to purchase another condo. Nobody knows where my mother lives at. When she left the projects she never looked back and I barely came around her, myself, let alone bring somebody with me. I'm spilling all the beans, giving up all the info. After all, my hands were clean.

Come to find out this wasn't a federal case; it was the state's responsibility. When I went downtown to the police station Swift was already a suspect and because I didn't have any concrete proof, nothing could be done. So now I'm back to square one with no Plan B.

Now I have to figure out what the hell I'm going to do. I can't take my mother for long. She gets on my last nerve…always has. Driving her car around wasn't doing me any justice either. *I can't be seen in a Ford Focus. This car is beneath me. It doesn't match my looks. I'm going to have to break down and buy myself a whip.* I called myself trying to sneak in the house, but as soon as I pulled up my mother was standing there in the door waiting for me. As If I didn't already have a bad day. *Here we go.* I was bracing myself.

*****

"You've been gone all damn day with my car. Why didn't you answer your phone?" My mother said with much attitude.

"Can I get in the door first before you start yelling? I figured you were sleeping, and my phone was on silent. By the time I looked and saw that you were calling, I was already on my way here." I lied. I saw her calling but I was busy taking care of business. She would just have to wait.

"We don't sleep all day around here. I work the overnight shift so that I can do my running around during the day. Now I can't get anything done. There is nothing in here for me to cook for dinner!" She threw her hands up in the air like that was supposed to make me feel some type of way.

"Ma, it's only four o'clock. You can still go to the store if you want." *I wish she would just shut up already.*

"Unlike you, I have to get me a couple of hours in before I go to work tonight. Speaking of work, are you looking for a job? We work around here. Everybody has to pay their way and you are not exempt."

"Well I don't plan on being here that long. I'm only here until I get back on my feet again." *Now she was irritating me.*

"I knew this day would come. We can't get you to come over here on a good day, but now that you're down and out you can come here. It doesn't work that way. When you were up driving around in your fancy car and living large no one heard from you. Then once that nigga dropped you like a bad habit you come knocking. I told you, you can't depend on a man. Lashay, you need to depend on yourself. We're your family and you shit on us! It's been plenty of times that I called you and asked you for twenty dollars and I couldn't get it. But I'm supposed to let you live here rent-free? I want four hundred a month or else you're getting out of here."

"Well, is my father still creeping around here? I'm pretty sure he can help out with my portion since he never did anything else for me." I said sarcastically. "If he pays then I will pay!"

"Lorenzo has nothing to do with you paying your way. You're a grown ass woman, not a child. Whatever he didn't do, I did. So if he owes anybody any type of money, it's me. Stop blaming that man for the wrong in your life. You're the way you are because you chose to be."

"Oh I don't just blame him. I blame you too. I watched you kiss that man's ass ever since I can remember. You worked your butt off for pennies while his wife sat on her pretty ass doing nothing. He comes knocking and you go spreading. You've spent all your life waiting on a man that you will never have. Hell no, I don't want to be like you! His other kids are living out in the county with their privileged lives while we were in the projects fighting roaches. We're standing at the bus stop, shivering in the cold and he riding by us with his wife and kids in a warm ass car with heat. We over here eating hot dogs and beans and they over there chewing on steak. I'm waving at the car yelling 'Daddy' and you smacking my hand down telling me to be quiet. That man would walk in and give me a kiss on the forehead and head straight to your bedroom. I don't even remember him saying 'Hello, How are you daughter?' Because he didn't give a damn. You two are the reason that I will never, ever push a baby out! Your children suffered because of a mistake that you made. You taught me everything not to be. That's why I'm the total opposite of you. You won't catch me in a kitchen slaving for a no show. You running around getting all dolled up for a man that can't even spend the night with you!" *Oh she's real mad now, she thinks she can smack me in my pretty face.* "Oh, you don't have any right putting your hands on me. You mad at me because you out here making women with a little bit of sense, a dose of self-esteem and some self-respect, look bad."

My mother grabbed me by the neck and started choking me as if I wasn't her daughter. "You little bitch! That's why I can't stand you."

I was trying to gasp for air when I lifted up my leg and kneed my mother in the stomach to get her off of me. While she was bent over trying to hold her stomach I jumped on her like she was a bitch in the street.

We were in the house rolling around like we were in a wrestling ring. I was trying to kill her and she was trying to kill me. *Here comes my brother Terrence to her rescue to break us up.* I wish he would have worked some overtime so I could whoop his mama's ass the way I really wanted to.

* * * * *

"Cut it out, now!" Terrance yelled as he was standing in-between us. *I wish his bitch ass would move.*

My mother was screaming, "I want this disrespectful ass whore out of my house right fucking now! From now on I don't have a daughter. You're dead to me!"

"Don't worry, I'm getting my stuff and getting the hell out of here. You just don't want to hear the truth!" I screamed trying to reach her head over Terrance so I could get one last hit in.

My mother swung and punched me in the face. Terrance picked me up and carried me outside to his car. "Let me go, put me down!" He pushed his weight on me so I couldn't move. *As soon as he lets up I'm running back up in there.* "Niecy is going to give me my belongings. She no longer deserves the respect of Mom. Fuck that!"

"You already know the drill. She's not going to let me take anything out of her house. I will get it later and bring it to you wherever you're at. Now get in the car." Terrance opened the car door so that I could get in. *She's lucky that he's here. She better count her blessings.*

"Where do you want me to bring you?" Terrance threw me my Michael Kors pocketbook.

"Bring me to the bank up the street and the BMW car dealership." I was happy that he had sense enough to grab it.

"Okay, sis you have to find a better way." Terrance shook his head like I was in the wrong.

"You sound just like your mother…crazy! I'm gonna hustle these niggas until I die." I jumped out the car and went into the bank and withdrew five thousand to put a down payment on my new car.

"Are you straight?" Terrance asked me as if I'm never not straight. Of course I'm going to always be straight.

"Yes, I'm good…as always!" I had to look at him sideways for asking me some dumb shit like that.

"I thought you told mom that you didn't have any money."

"I don't have any money for Niecy. I have enough for me to survive off of."

"Where are you going to stay at?" Terrance was being nosey but I'm not telling him anything so he can run back and tell his mother.

"I'll stay in my car if I have to, but I'm going to be just fine. You watch! I'm sick of your mother. She couldn't even help me out for five minutes. She always asking me for money, but dad gets to ride her ass for free!"

"Lala, stop it! You can't stay nowhere for free. Them niggas got you spoiled. There is a such thing as rent, gas, electric, water, and food bill. I give mom money every week."

"Yeah and you're too old to be home with mommy. You should have your own place by now and a better ride. I don't know how you keep a chick. Nevermind, they're just like your mother, so they will go for anything."

"I see why Mom punched you in your face. Your mouth is reckless. Unlike you, I have kids to feed and take care of. I take care of my responsibilities and I'm not out here slinging drugs so I can be locked up and not see my seeds."

"That's what happens when you have kids, slows you down. How come you always take her side like you didn't go through the same things that I did? You and Bo never stuck up for me."

"Regardless, she's our mother. There's this thing called respect that I was raised with. Not sure where you came from."

"There's a saying that goes a little something like this, 'in order to get respect you have to give it' and I don't care who you are. When you have a mother that called her daughter all kinds of bitches and whores since the age of five, you tend to forget that you came out her pussy. I get more respect out here in these streets than I ever did from her." I wasn't getting anywhere with this conversation. I never could get through to my brothers, so why start now?

"She only says those things when she's mad at you. That's just how she is." Terrence shrugged his shoulders like that made it right.

"You have a five year old daughter. What could she possibly do to make you disrespect her like that? Tell me bro, I'm listening, my ears are wide open. That's what I thought, not a damn thing."

"All I'm saying is that she's our mother and she did take care of us. Just take from all the positive that she taught us, not the negative."

I had to laugh; old bro had become a comedian. "What positive? You know what the woman taught me? Do you really want to hear it, brace yourself Bro. Number one, never fuck for free; this jewel that I carry in between my legs is one powerful bitch. Number two, never settle for the side dish; I'm always gonna be the main. Number three, never work a nine to five; shit ain't worth it. Number four, never to let a man fuck over me; he's only going to do what I allow him to do. Number five, never get strung out on the dick; I control the dick, not let the dick control me. Number six, never put my all in one man; everything in life is temporary. Number seven, never let my emotions get the best of me; always think with my head because I'm heartless. Number eight, never overlook myself; I come first at all costs; selfish is a good thing. Number nine, never let him know that I have a dollar; always cry broke. The more the merrier. Number ten, never fall in love; it represents a weak bitch! So now you have the Ten Commandments of a Female Hustler!"

CHAPTER 18

JAY

$\mathcal{M}$y life was going very good and I was embracing the change. L.A. was surely my new home; much different from Baltimore. Boss was taking me to another level; I never had a man so caring and thoughtful like him. Date night was beautiful. He took me out on a horse and buggy ride. We rode all around town. I thought this kind of stuff only happened in the movies. He took me to Oliver's, a five star restaurant where most celebrities go. We sat in a private area; I liked it because nobody bothered us. The candles were lit, rose pedals spread out…it was very romantic.

After dinner we went back to the hotel. Boss got the suite for the night. When he opened the door there were two beds laid out for us to get full body massages. I fell asleep. It felt so good. *I really could get used to this life.* To top the night off it was really regular.

Most times when we went out there's always Paparazzi taking pictures, fans wanting to take pictures with him, handing him demo's, performing for him. Sometimes it could get to be a bit much. Thank God I'm not the jealous type and I live in tough skin because these women are ruthless. They would run up to him, kiss him, hug him, damn near try and strip for him. He always handled them well without pissing them off. They always ignored me; I guess because I'm not famous.

Of course, just like any relationship, there were a few things that bothered me. One was whenever he does his radio or magazine interviews, he lies and says that he's single. Then I overheard him arguing with somebody on the phone and I could have sworn he said something about his kids that I'm unaware of. I don't know how to approach that conversation because I was eavesdropping. I don't want to give him no reason not to trust me. If he does have kids, then the situation will present itself again and that's when I will go from there. Other than that, we were getting along just fine.

We finally found a house to rent that we both liked, or should I say, that he liked. They were all nice to me. While he's out working I'm busy decorating and getting things in the house in order. We decided on a five bedroom, five and a half bath, indoor/outdoor pool. The house had a studio in it so that he could work from home sometimes. It was in a gated community. The home was beautiful, something that I could only dream of living in.

Boss landed me my first gig for his girl group called Unique. It was three young ladies and they had to do a video shoot this weekend so I would be quite busy doing their make-up. I'm so excited; I can't wait to meet them in person. Hopefully once word gets out, I'll have more opportunities. I'm finally going to be making my own money.

My cooking wasn't up to par, so I started watching all the cooking shows. I wanted to be able to cook for Boss. I called Grams on a regular to coach me through, but lately it was two to three times a day. She knew how to cook from scratch. All the years she's been cooking, I should have had my behind in the kitchen learning a thing or two instead of being in the streets. I actually like cooking now that I'm trying to perfect it. I think Boss was getting spoiled. He wasn't even mentioning going out to eat. Lately, he just calls to see what's on the menu. It's funny to me; I'm starting to feel like I'm somebody's wife.

*****

I looked down at my phone and Jock had called me ten times. *I wonder what he wants; I haven't spoken to him since I left without a trace.* Then I looked at the text that read 'Call me, 911.' *Okay, so now I know something is going on, but it better not be about Lala and her drama.*

"Hey what's up?"

"Binky is locked the fuck up. That's what's up!" Jock said with straight attitude. "Answer your damn phone, fuck that nigga!"

"My phone wasn't near me, what happened?" My heart dropped. *I told her to stay out of trouble she knows she has time over her head.*

"She went to see her probation officer last week and they locked her up. Yo, they had all kinds of pics of you and her gallivanting from city to city. That's why I don't post any pics and I stay the hell away from any type of social media. That shit makes you hot. Anyway, she called Moose and told him to get in touch with you. She has no bail and we're waiting on a court date."

"I'm telling you right now that Lala's name is written all over this. Now what?"

"Now we play the waiting game, but most likely she's not getting out. Moose said that Bink said the same thing you just said. Lala did this shit. She ain't nowhere to be found, but she can't hide forever."

"Trust me, she ain't hiding. The bitch is ruthless. She's around somewhere. Can you tell Moose to tell Binky to call me? She has five years hanging over her head. This is not right at all. There has to be some way that we can get her out of there, but now I'm afraid of what she might do to Lala and end up right back in there." Binky wouldn't be on probation if she wasn't fighting Lala's battles. This was lower than her trying to holla at Boss-man.

"Yeah, I'll tell him. So what's up with you? Is he treating you right?"

"Yes, much better than you." I let that slip. "I mean…"

"Naw, you said it just the way you meant it. It's cool though, I'm not stressing. Just hope it stays that way. We men tend to be one way until we get you, then once we got ya, shit switches up. Remember that. But I'm here for you when you need me. Look out for that phone call." Jock hung up the phone.

*****

I really want to call this bitch and cuss her out but what was the use. Home girl was lost and forgot all about loyalty. Binky did all her dirt for her. Lala was always having a problem with somebody and Bink would handle that shit. Put Binky in a ring and all bets were on her even when it came down to niggas. *Her hand game was stupid. Now what was the beautiful Ms. Lashay gonna do? Who was gonna have her back?* She might just get fucked up just because I'm gone and Binky is locked up. *Yep, she had trouble on her hands.*

Lala was the most hated female in the streets, but nobody would touch her because nobody wanted to feel the wrath of Bink. *Let's see who protects that ass now.* To make things a little better, she no longer had Swift's protection either.

The streets had a lot of respect for him too. But now she's all uncovered, left out there wide open. I hope she's ready for what she's in for.

I just need to talk to Binky. I know how she can get, especially when she don't have a care in the world. I know she can handle herself in there physically, but mentally, Bink struggled in that department. Being locked down for five years just might break her...not to mention other charges that she would catch while in there. *I'm gonna have to make frequent visits back home.* She needs me now and I have to go and check up on Grams. I have nobody to do her grocery shopping or go to the corner store for her. *I might just have to pay Binks' uncle to do it for a while.* If the money was right, I know for a fact that he would have no problem running a couple of errands. He was just nosy as hell. I know that Boss-man will help in any way that he can. *Maybe he has some connections there.* Money talks and bullshit always walks. I stand by that. If a lawyer could find any glitch in the system, then Bink could walk.

CHAPTER 19

LALA

Thank goodness for the devil putting this master plan all up in my head. I'm about to be on, this come up will be like no other. Sometimes all you have to do is sit back and think with a clear head. When nothing works in your favor, you have to make it work in your favor. Boss-man chose Jay over me, Bink ran her mouth to Swift, the feds shut me down, the state shut me down, mom put her hands on me, brothers never had my back, daddy watched me suffer, Swift turned on me, and Diamond has always been an enemy of mine; now this bitch thinks that she has the upper hand. *Let the games begin.*

*****

First on my to-do list was to have my meeting with Rock, Tiz's cousin, over south Baltimore. At first he didn't want anything to do with me. Dude never liked me in the first place, so it was hard getting him to meet me. I guess he thought that I was trying to set him up or something.

Truth be told, he's still a little leery of me. But I know he will have plenty of security around him. I told him that I had pertinent information for him regarding Tiz, so the love he had for his cousin outweighed any personal beef that he had with me.

Tiz was on the up and up, but most of his family wasn't. Rock had the south side on lock down. That was his territory. Now this could kind of backfire on me but my phony tears and need for protection just might help along the way.

*****

I pulled up at the pit beef spot he told me to meet him at and just like I thought, dudes in black all over the place, covering every corner just waiting for some shit to pop off. As soon as I stepped out of my BMW, I was being patted down by two of them who were actually enjoying patting me on my ass. I just smiled and walked in.

"Have a seat, Lala," Rock was sitting at the table.

I walked over and sat across from him. He was staring at me with his fist up by his mouth. "Hi Rock, how are you?"

"Bitch, get to the point. You know I don't do no small talk! What's this information that you have on Tiz?"

"Swift did it. I'm running scared out here. We broke up because I just couldn't be with him knowing that he killed Tiz for no reason." I let my phony tears begin to run down my face.

"The only thing that you're telling me that I don't know is that you and Swift broke up. The streets talk; I know he did it. I also know that you never stopped messing with Tiz either. You were at his house a couple days before he got killed. I already put one and two together. Swift found out and took Tiz out, but my question to you is, why are you still breathing? You come in here all crying and shit like I give a fuck about any of your tears!"

"How do you know that I was with Tiz?" I took a tissue to wipe my tears.

"I'm asking the questions, not you! I don't know why you brought your dumb ass over here in the first place!"

"Rock, I was leaving Swift that night. Me and Tiz were going to run off and get married. I was tired of being abused by Swift. He's crazy! I don't know how he found out; all I know is that he dragged me out of that club with his gun pointed at my back. I tried to run back in the club, but it was too late. Shots had already been fired. Swift threatened to throw me off our balcony if I left him." *I hope these lies work.*

"Well, why didn't he? Your story isn't quite adding up! You was scared to leave then, but now you're not? You grew balls overnight and decided to break up and he just let you walk away, just like that!"

"I took off for a weekend to get away from him. When I came back he moved his side bitch in. He took my condo and the car he bought for me and gave it to her. The only reason he didn't throw me off that balcony is because he saw that the pregnancy test was positive. I'm pregnant, but I think that this baby belongs to Tiz. Swift and I weren't sleeping together like that." Rock looked at me as if he was starting to believe me.

"You're real lucky right now, because I had no intentions on letting you walk out of here alive. All of that changes when you might be pregnant with my bloodline in you. If I could take the baby out of you and let him or her live, then I would, but since I can't, your life will be spared for now."

"Thank you, Rock! That's why I wanted to tell you. All I ask, either way this goes, Swift has to die for what he did to Tiz. I won't rest well until he's dead and gone! I'm willing to help you in any way that I can. I know his whereabouts."

"I know his whereabouts too. Trust me, I got this and I don't need any help from you. When the time is right, he won't be here! For now you just keep watching the news and if things get a little tricky out here, just give me a call. I don't want nothing happening to you or that baby, now get out of here! I will be in touch from time to time."

I don't know what signal Rock gave his boys, but when I got outside and hit the alarm on my car, one of the guys that patted me down a little while ago opened up my car door and closed it for me. He even had the nerve to say 'Drive safely beautiful.' *Well I'm glad I made it out of there safely. I almost want to pat myself on the back.*

CHAPTER 20

SWIFT

I opened the door for Moose and Jock. It was time for our monthly meeting, along with a smoke session so we can just chill and get fucked up. Diamond will be gone for a while. She knows what time it is.

"What's up fellas?" I gave them dap. "Have a seat and let's get this party started. Moose, spark that blunt up over there on the table."

"Alright, alright, that's what's up!" Moose sparked it up.

"We took a major hit this month. There's been a decrease in sales and I think it's because all of us are still laying low." I'm never happy about losing money. "Now I know we got new head men in charge. Are y'all sure that they are on the up and up?"

"Well numbers don't lie and the product is counted up. I haven't had any shorts. Everything has been coming in just as it should. My men are handling theirs." Jock coughed and passed the blunt to me.

"Yeah, same here." Moose was in agreement with Jock.

"Alright, well we will just see how we do next month and go from there. We might have to implement some changes. Are we good on the product, Jock?"

"Yeah, we good; same order, same supplier. It's scheduled to be delivered any day now. I'm expecting a call from UNC any day now."

"Good." Sometimes I have to remind Jock because he gets a little side tracked every now and then, instead of always being about his business.

"Moose, do we have adequate security in-place for the drop, whenever Jock gets that call?"

"You already know that I have Plan B and C in place, just in case A falls through. Don't worry; I got this. Everybody knows what to do when they get that text."

"My man, is there any other business that we need to discuss?" *Something about Moose seems a little off.*

"Yeah, I have a question. When do you plan on taking care of your situation out here? I mean, we can't hide out forever."

"I haven't pin-pointed out exactly who is looking for me. Usually by now word is out, but nobody's giving me anything.

Whoever is after me is being mighty quiet right now. I've been waiting, so I can make a move. Right now I'm stuck."

"I haven't heard anything either, but that tells me that they're planning to do something on the sneak. Anytime the streets are quiet like this, somebody has their thinking cap on and it's going to be very well planned out. Just a heads up, I'm gonna beef up some more security, so take that into account for next months profit." Moose lit up another blunt.

"Oh well, we have to do what we have to for now." Nervous ain't never really been in my blood. Moose is more worried than me.

"How's it going since you been here with Diamond?" Jock asked me.

"Diamond is a diamond, best decision I ever made. She's in here making a nigga happy every day. This place stays clean. Isabelle comes and looks around like 'damn I don't have nothing to do.' I'm getting breakfast and full course dinner meals. We order out once a week and that's because I tell her to take a day off. When I'm out, she makes me want to come home to her. We be in here laughing and talking. She's not worried about the latest fashion that's coming out. I know the strippers miss my weekly visit, but I have no need when I have my own strip show at home. I'm thinking about changing her last name, for real." *I can't tell them about my new tattoo just yet, I can't deal with hearing Moose's mouth.*

"Yo, you heard from that other one?" Moose was asking about the infamous Lala.

"Nope, and I like it that way. I forgot to tell y'all what the bitch did to the Bentley. Well, she smeared blood all on the driver's side and spray painted it. Diamond was pissed. She calmed down a little bit for now. Lala is in for it when Diamond does see her. This is the one time having insurance came in handy; I only had to pay the deductible. We got the car back last week from the shop."

"That's some foul shit right there but I'm glad you got rid of that bitch. I bet them pockets are a lot fatter too. You need to slow down though on that last name thing, nigga. You starting to sound a little whipped. What we look like being somebody's husband when we out here wheeling and dealing? Save that shit for when you get old and dick is barely getting up." Moose had jokes but it was some truth in what he was saying. I can't even be mad at him.

"Yeah man, I'm happy for you. Don't listen to Moose, do what your heart says do. I can't wait to be a best man in the wedding. Moose got a fucked up way of thinking when it comes down to these women. I could have married Jay if I would have done right by her. I wish Tracey did something with herself, besides whine and complain about this pregnancy. The shit is starting to stress me out. She can't wait for the baby to come and neither can I."

"You hear this shit, Swift? This nigga wasn't thinking about marrying nobody until she upped and left his ass alone. Jay had that nigga over there singing Mr. Telephone Man; he was all in his feelings. I walk up on him late night while he's sitting in the car and he in there singing to them slow jams. He was heartbroken. This fool ain't never been on a plane in his life and all of a sudden he was ready to fly somewhere like she was coming back with him. Jay went and found her a baller that can take her places other than Baltimore City and this fool was ready to cry. He had a million opportunities to put a bitch in a better situation and he mad. He traded her in for a washed up Tracey; a chick that he can't even bring outside or be seen with. Where they do that at? I hope that baby looks like you because other than that you won't be able to find uncle, I'm gonna always be busy." *Moose is stupid as shit, he got me in tears right now. I don't think Jock is finding Moose clowning his ass funny.*

"Alright fellas, meeting adjourned. Y'all done smoked up all my shit, now get the hell out of here!"

CHAPTER 21

JAY

"*H*ey Binky," I was relieved to finally be hearing from her.

"Hey Jay, what's going on?" Binky sounded like she wanted to cry.

"What's going on with you? I have been worrying myself sick."

"I have to get out of here, Jay. This shit ain't no joke. I've been in here fighting day and night. They transferred me to Uptown; these chicks in here look like straight up dudes. My first day here I ended up in the hole. This chick grabbed my ass and hemmed me up against the wall. She tried to kiss me. I had to go buck wild. You have to earn respect in here. I don't like being in the population. The hole is the best place for me. Only thing is, I don't get to make any phone calls. So don't worry about me when you don't hear from me; just know that's where I'm at."

"What can I do? I feel so helpless." I didn't want to get Binky's hopes up, but Boss-man was working on something. Just like she thought, he knew people and was willing to help.

"I'm just waiting on a court date; there isn't much anyone can do. My public defender ain't shit though. He just goes with whatever the state says. I need a lawyer, Jay, and a good one."

"I got you. I'm already working on it. The lawyer that Boss-man is talking to went and got your file from the public defender. We're just waiting to hear back from him. I'm coming up for your court date. So put me on the visitor's list."

"Awww, thank you Jay. I feel so much better. At least now I have a real lawyer on my side. See if he can get me transferred out of here. At the rate I'm going, I'm not gonna be able to have any visits as long as I keep getting in trouble. They look at me like I'm a piece of meat. I'm not going out like that; not without a fight."

"Yeah all they see is this pretty girl locked down with them. They weren't expecting you to be able to hold your own." *I'm worried about Binky's well being in there. Boss has to do something.*

"Yeah, I'm hanging in there, but I can't fight all these women in here by myself. I'm gonna have to take a side. Meaning, I'm gonna have to join one of these gangs in here. The streets are safer than being in here. As much as I want to do Lala dirty when I get out of here, she ain't even worth it. Thanks for the money; I'm assuming that it came from you. A lot of these women don't have anybody so I can buy my way in for a minute."

"You're welcome, if I have it then so do you. No need to thank me. If the tables were turned you would do the same for me." I was relieved that Binky wasn't going to retaliate on Lala but I can't promise that I won't.

"The phone is getting ready to cut off. I love you girl, and I'll try and give you a call as soon as I can."

"I love you too. I'll be waiting on my phone call from you." The phone disconnected. I screamed out loud to let some frustration out. Oh my God, life was getting crazier and crazier.

*****

I was starting to realize that I didn't really know Boss-man. His presentation was on point but he was a liar in disguise. I was wondering why we needed a five bedroom when it was just us two. It was quiet and peaceful for a quick minute. As soon as I got the house together here came his entourage partying every night.

The house was full of all these thirsty ho's and whores freeloading. I'm in here cooking for us and the food was being demolished by his crew. It took the joy out of cooking for me. *Why cook if I'm never going to be able to sit down and eat it myself?* Now we're back to ordering out every night which doesn't seem to bother Boss in the least.

The house was tore up from the floor up every day. All you saw was empty bottles, cups and glasses everywhere. I was finding used condom wrappers spread out all through the house. A bunch of pill popping, weed heads and cocaine users, that's all they were. Our house was just like them hotel rooms. It was starting to get to me, but I just pictured me going back to where I came from; anything beat that. I would go in my gigantic room shut the door and block it all out. I was confined to the room at night, just me and my thoughts, until Boss decided that he was tired enough to come to bed. *If I have to pacify this situation until I get established and get Binky straight then that's what I will do.*

*****

I was so excited to be doing the make-up for Unique, until I felt the disrespect. Boss didn't tell me that they were used to this other make-up artist named Tiffany, so they treated me like shit the whole time. I was there until they saw my work. After that they loosened up a little.

This industry was straight cut throat. You better be able to swim because they don't have no problem throwing you in a bunch of dirty ass water to drown. It's good money in it, but they treated me like I was the enemy. I had no idea what I was walking in on, and Boss didn't feel the need to fill me in or give me a clue. That was the longest twelve hours of my life. All I got was straight attitude, but I took that seven G's. That's the most money I ever made in my life and it was mine. The group was far from happy, even the director felt sorry for me. His name was Kenny; he was trying to look out for me.

I've always been good at what I do but these chicks weren't trying to budge. I made a little leeway with the lead singer, if that's what you call it. She did mumble a thank you to me when I was leaving.

Boss let me see pictures of them beforehand so I already had their faces visualized in my head as to how I wanted them to look. I had already critiqued this Tiffany characters style and I knew I had one up on her. It took the pics to hit the gram in order for them to give me a little bit of respect.

My schedule could be booked but Boss was only letting me go but so far. He was stopping my flow; I guess he figured that if I got too big in this industry that I would leave him. I'm loyal by default. I guess he doesn't see that in me yet. Because of everything that he has done for me, gratefulness would always be in my heart. That's just me; life has taught me to never forget where you come from because you just might find yourself right back in that same spot. That is where my endurance for the bullshit comes in at. *Aww man somebody is ringing the doorbell. Why do we live in a gated community if everybody can get past the guards?*

*****

"Who is it?" *I should have just turned the camera on so that I could see.* It's some chick that I never seen before. She's tall, light brown; her hair is in a nice ponytail. A nice looking older lady. *Probably one of the groupies that's too old to still be stalking a celebrity.* I open the door, "Whoever you're looking for is not here, this is not party hour."

"Are you sure?" She barges in looking around. "This is quite nice, a bit messy though! Y'all need a maid up in here."

"Who are you looking for and who told you to barge in here like you the motherfucking police?" I jumped in her face ready for whatever.

"Um, little girl, please take a step back before you end up not being so pretty. I just wanted to see who was taking care of my husband these days. What's your name and how old are you?"

Okay now she just went left on me. She has got to go. "I think it's time for you to leave Miss whoever you are."

"Oh let me introduce myself, how rude of me. I'm Mrs. Brock." This woman had the nerve to be smiling at me. "Oh! Boss didn't tell you that he had a wife and kids? I'm not surprised, he likes to keep secrets."

"Wife?" *She can't be serious right now.* "Well if you're his wife then where have you and these kids been?"

"We've been together for twelve years, married for five and separated for the last two. I'm no threat to you; I don't want him. I'm just tired of taking care of these kids; I need a break. I will be leaving them here with you." *Oh my God! Did she just sit on the couch trying to make herself comfortable.*

"Excuse me; I'm so confused right now." *I don't know whether I'm coming or going right now; I can't raise no kids.*

"What's to be confused about? I just told you what you needed to know. Oh, I do have to introduce you to my kids; they're sitting in the car. I'll go get them in a few minutes."

"Are you on drugs or something? You can't just come and drop off kids that I don't even know and expect me to raise them." *She has to be smoking something.*

"I know I just dropped a bomb on you, but you will be okay. No, I'm not on drugs. What's your name and cell phone number so that I can check on them from time to time? I'll be in and out, not like I'm going to be a dead beat mother."

*****

I looked at her like she had ten heads with my mouth wide open in disbelief. *This was some shit right here. I must be having a nightmare and getting ready to wake up at any minute. Am I watching her wave to the kids, and do I see two little girls plus a boy running up in here?*

"Hey kids, this is daddy's little girlfriend. She's going to be watching you for a while. Mommy will call y'all real soon. Don't let anything happen to my kids. I would hate to have to kill your ass." She left just like that.

CHAPTER 22

LALA

*T*his week has been very hectic for me. I finally closed on my condo that I bought in Canton for a pretty decent price. I ended up putting sixty thousand dollars down, which damn near killed me to take out the bank. That was the only way the bank would approve my loan because of my lack of employment. My self-employment lies worked out for me in the end though. I had to purchase all new furniture; bad enough I was still trying to build up my wardrobe.

I spent thousands staying in hotels. *I need my money to grow not dwindle. All of this because of punk ass Swift, not to mention he was still among the living. I wish Rock would hurry up and just off him already.*

I saw the Bentley again and tore that the fuck up. Busted out the windows and flattened the tires, but still no Diamond in sight. I couldn't wait for her after making all that noise, I had to haul ass before the cops came.

*****

I pulled up to finally be meeting up with Sweets, which was a job in itself. I had to woo my way to him; beauty pays off. I had to go through this one and that one.

He ran the west side but it was hard catching up to him, and by me not having any contact information made it extra hard. You would think that he would at least checkup on things every now and then, but that's not how he operated his business. I guess he trusted his lieutenants and sergeants to do the job for him. All he did was run the organization. Swift, Jock, and Moose were peons compared to him.

I was finally able to set up a meeting with him after being given the run around for three days. I saw him walking up to my car with his hood-rat girlfriend, Nina. *Oh, I forgot how ugly Sweets was.* I have no idea how he got that name when he looked worse than Flava Flav, but his money was almost as long as old money. That had to be the only reason why Nina was with him. She kind of reminded me of a Halle Berry; just a tad bit under me, and my beautiful self. I don't blame her though, with money that long, you don't see any looks. I can definitely relate to her.

*****

Sweets knocked on my window; I rolled it down. "I heard you been looking for me, so what's up? How can I help a pretty lady like you?"

"You can start by getting in the car. I promise I won't bite you." I just had to flirt a little bit.

"There ain't nothing wrong with biting; now, I usually don't do this but for you I will." He walked over to the passenger seat and got in the car. Nina was standing outside like a little puppy waiting to bark.

"I need your help and I have a business proposition for you." *Please let this work for me.*

"What kind of help?" He touched my face.

"Well, I know you heard about Swift getting caught up in that Tiz situation."

"Yeah, I heard a little something, but what does that have to do with me?"

"Well, Swift's supplier will no longer be supplying to him. He's going to need a supplier. Unfortunately, his connection was related to Tiz somehow. That supplier could be you, just think about how much money you could make."

"Now I know exactly who you are, you're his girl. I knew you looked familiar; I just couldn't put my finger on it. I haven't heard anything like that. We both respect each other's territories. Swift will never agree to buy anything from me; I'm the competition. Are you trying to cause a war? You're wasting my time with this nonsense. I don't know who you think I am, but Sweets don't play these types of games. As beautiful as you are, you can disappear if you know what I mean. It's best that you pull off and don't come back around here. I will forget that we ever had this conversation."

"Sweets, listen to me please. I'm no longer with Swift; he did me real dirty so I have a vengeance to repay. I didn't come all the way over here for three days straight looking for you, to tell you a lie. Now I need money, he won't know that you're the one supplying him unless you say something to the wrong person. You can damn near triple your money by doing this!"

"Wait a minute; now how do you get paid off of this? I don't want anything to do with a love affair that went wrong; that's not my line of work." I could tell Sweets was thinking about it, even though he was portraying like he wasn't.

"I get paid off the transaction; you give me a cut off the money that you make. I'm telling you that I can make this happen and we both win."

"Sweetheart, I'm a huge fan of loyalty and you don't have any. If you could turn on a man that you supposedly have loved, then what makes me any different? You can't be trusted. I have my business to the point where it's being run at a smooth pace."

"I never told you that I loved the man. I don't know what it is to love another human being, but I do know what it is to love money. I have respect for people. He wasn't loyal to me either, as you can see. I'm not hurting him by getting my hustle on; actually I'm still helping him. He will never get a better deal than what you can offer him. He's too stupid to even step your way but I'm smart enough to."

"Okay, I will think about it, but I have some conditions! In order for me to think about it, I need a threesome with you and my girl." He pointed to Nina.

"Uh and when would you like this?" *Sweets threw me for a loop on this one. I wasn't expecting that.*

"Like, right now. My dick is hard from looking at you. I can't wait for you to get out of this car so I can see what kind of an ass you working with. You look like you have nice big nipples too. I can tell from the imprint on your shirt. I want to fuck the shit out of that pussy. I'm gonna go fill Nina in on what might go down but don't take too long getting that ass out the car either. I've never been the patient type when I want to fuck, and I want to fuck!"

CHAPTER 23

SWIFT

"*Y*o, what the fuck happened?" Moose just jumped in my car.

"Niggas came from out of nowhere and just started shooting up the whole block. That's all I know right now!"

"Is everybody okay or is somebody down?"

"I think it's three down; two in critical, one that got grazed by a bullet. I can't find out shit. They want you to sign in and niggas is up in Union Memorial on that John Doe mess. I went by there earlier but the cops are everywhere up in there. I'm waiting to hear something and I'm trying to take a tally. Swift, I had coverage all over the place…they were just too quick for us."

"Moose, you slipping man! Why didn't you have some parked cars sitting around in the area loaded up? When you knew we needed extra security you don't just order for more niggas to pile up on the block; you got to have all that shit covered. I depend on you man. You tell me how the fuck, in broad daylight, they can drive down a busy street, that we run, and shoot up and down the damn block? Who you got hiding in the vacant houses? You mean they didn't see anything either? Bullshit! I'm no fool; it's a glitch in the loyalty and it's coming from our end."

"Let's not jump to conclusions without having the facts. We need to narrow this down. We have no beef with the west side at all. Sweets always send a warning before he strikes. This can't be coming from the north side because they use us to supply them from time to time. They wouldn't take a chance. The only person that leaves is Rock, who's known for acting in silence."

"I grew up hanging around Rock, he didn't do this. Rock is not going to shoot up a whole block of unknowns. He comes after exactly who he's looking for. I can't pin this on him. You just said Sweets always sends a warning, and I think he just sent it."

"Swift, that makes no sense. We don't have any beef with that man anymore. I don't want to strike back and we end up striking wrong. Then we start a war that never needed to be started and we're not strong enough to handle all of that right now. The boys just proved that to us."

"We need to be strong enough to handle anything that comes our way. This shit right here can't happen again. I hear what you saying but listen to me; if we don't strike back by the end of the week, then we have just set up ourselves as the weakest east side ever. So you choose what angle we're going in on. Somebody has to catch it! Where the hell is Jock? He needs to be in on this."

"Oh yeah! I forgot to tell you; Tracey went into labor so he's a Hopkins waiting for the baby to come. Tell me why Diamond is in a rental again? What happened to the car now?"

"Lala busted out the windows and flattened the tires. Once I handle some of this business, then I'm going to handle her. If she keeps fucking with me she's gonna find herself right with old boy."

"Again, why does she keep fucking with the car? Just give Diamond a fair one!"

"Yeah Diamond's been looking for her. I'm tired of her Moose! My whole thing is this, how the hell are you gonna be mad about a condo that you never put a dime in? A car that she ain't never put a dime in? She didn't even pay for gas to drive the bitch. She had a whole free ride for the last three years. Anything that she asked for, I gave it to her. She had the world in her hands and it still wasn't enough. What woman out here would fuck some shit up like that? I worked my ass off to get here, she didn't! The bitch acts like I owe her something; I can't owe you if I never borrowed shit from you. I'm not saying that I was a saint, but Diamond wouldn't have had the chance to get any of my time if she even acted like she cared about something other than the dollars in my pocket. Every other day this bitch needed money for something. Diamond is quick to say 'Baby, I don't need that; save your money.' When I come home, Diamond asks me how my day was. I'm trying to figure out how I put up with her so long. When she took off for that weekend I knew it was over.

I got a queen right now that I crowned to sit on the throne. My eyes don't wander because I have it all at home."

"I feel you. That is exactly why I can't let a bitch get me caught up. You and Jock can have all of that. You don't ever hear me complaining; I shut them down real quick. If I got to pay for pussy then I might as well do just that. I'm cool with Bink. We have an understanding. Because she is the way she is, I don't mind giving her a couple dollars here and there. She rides for me and I ride for her. She told me straight up that she was feeling some dude and its okay. I know I'm not ready, so why hold onto her; giving her false hopes? I let shawty do her thing. I let her know I'm not going anywhere; if she needs me, just call me. You know me Swift, I ain't playing no games with these females out here."

"Yeah, Lala had me caught up for a long minute. I was sleep, but I'll be damned if I'm not wide awake now."

"Let's go check in and see our brother; welcome his seed into this world. We need a change of thought right now."

"Yep, sounds like a plan to me; let's roll Moose!"

CHAPTER 24

JAY

"*J*ay, can I talk to you for a minute?"

I was working on the set. Tweeny, a female rapper, had contacted her last minute to do her make-up for her video shoot. Her make-up artist had canceled so she called her up. Of course I said yes. I got the hell out of that house and away from the bae bae kids. *Now here Boss-man comes thinking that he's going to interrupt my work. What's he doing here anyway? He can wait until I finish.* "I'm working right now." I was concentrating on beating Tweeny's face.

"I'll wait until you finish."

It was thirty minutes of me wishing that Tweeny didn't have to go do her first take because I really didn't feel like talking to him.

"Come here." Boss-man pulled me to the side. "What's up? It seems like you've been trying to avoid me."

"I really don't have much to say to you these days." I was being very standoffish.

"I apologized to you. What can I do to make this right? I don't like us right now. I want us to get back like it was before." Boss put my hands in his looking me straight in my eyes.

I snatched my hands back. "That's kind of hard to do when you never told me about a wife and kids."

"Okay, I get that. I haven't been with her in two years. You're acting like I cheated on you."

"No, you just lied; which means you're capable of cheating. Those two go hand in hand. You had more than enough time to tell me. How long were you planning to carry on this charade?"

"I was waiting for the right time. I wanted to tell you, but Tasha just came and dropped the kids off. I still can't believe she did that. This is not how I wanted you to find out."

"No, I should have found out day one. Now I have to second guess myself about what's real and fake."

"What's real is that I love you and want you to be a part of my life. Why would I move you all the way here for something superficial? I deal with that all day every day. I could have any one of these women." Boss-man pointed around. "I chose to be with you!"

"When is she coming back to pick up the kids? That's all I want to know." *I'm tired of them disrespecting me every chance they get. I'm two seconds away from whooping ass.*

"I don't know. She's not returning my calls. Hopefully it won't be too much longer."

"Well now that you have your kids in the house, the partying needs to stop. They don't need to be around that and since you don't know when your wife is going to return, you need to enroll them in school…like yesterday. She didn't pack them enough clothes; you need to take them shopping. I'll do the girls' hair later on when I get home. Please take Kyle to your barber; he needs a haircut."

Boss-man was grinning from ear to ear. "So you're gonna stick by me? You just gave me a shit load of stuff to do."

"I'm trying to help you. I may not have any kids, but I do know what they need. I'm sticking by you for now, but if another bomb drops on me then I'm out. My love for you and no amount of money will keep me." I walked away to watch Tweeny doing her shoot.

*****

The video shoot went well. Tweeny and I got along really well. Tweeny was so impressed with my talent that she decided to use me for her next two videos, one was in Saint Marten, but that would be a while. All expenses paid, plus it was extra money for me. So of course I said yes. *Hopefully the kids will be gone by then.*

In between takes I was able to get in touch with Bink's lawyer; he said he was still working on a date, but he did manage to have

Binky moved to another facility that would be more suitable for her. *That would explain why I haven't heard from her.* He said that she should be calling soon. He met with her a couple of times to discuss her case and was hopeful that he could get her out on house arrest. It was better than nothing. That made my day knowing that my girl was alright.

Now I have to head home to these hateful ass kids. Boss' children were of a different breed. I had to respect my elders, that's the way my grandmother raised me. Shayla, the oldest, was eleven the other day. I was in the kitchen trying to heat up some left overs when she just started squirting ketchup all over me and thought it was funny. Kyle is nine, and he thought it was okay to kick me whenever he felt like it. The baby, Ashley, well she's only seven and just as sweet as she can be. So lovable. It's just the other two demon seeds that I can't deal with.

They were always doing something. Boss was hardly ever home. What was the point of having a studio in the house if he was never going to use it? *That's just another thing for me to add to the list. He has to spend some quality time with his kids.* Since they have been here, he acts like he doesn't want to be bothered either. Everything wasn't going to be on me. I think that they're missing a lack of love and attention. I don't think their mother did much with them. *I know how that feels.* I always felt unloved, even though I knew my grandmother loved me. She couldn't really take me out and do things with me. She was old and fragile. I missed out on a lot as a kid. I wanted to go to the park and swing on swings. I wanted to go to a carnival or amusement park, and still to this day I haven't. *Maybe I will take the kids and get on some rides with them.*

One good thing about them being with us is that now I have an opportunity to do some things that I've always wanted to do. I've never even stepped foot in a church, not even for a funeral. All the ones that I went to were in funeral homes. My grandmother didn't even have a bible like most families did. My upbringing was strange; just like these kids, but if I could save them from going through some of what I went through then I will.

CHAPTER 25

LALA

$\mathcal{A}$fter I followed through with the threesome with Sweets and Nina I thought that I had fulfilled my end of the bargain; I was wrong. Sweets had other plans for me. He wanted me to learn the business and then he would see if he would work with me. I was sure that once I put it on him that I could seal the deal. For the first time in my life my pussy had failed me.

*****

I worked that graveyard shift for two weeks with no pay, but I racked in quite a few dollars ranging anywhere from two to five G's a day that I had to hand over to the Sweets' Lieutenant. Not bad for an eight hour shift, and that's with people being skeptical about buying from me. They weren't used to a woman being out here working this block. I put my hat on, no make-up and bought myself some sweat suits; something that I never wear. I didn't want to bring too much attention to myself.

Sweets' other workers weren't too thrilled to have me out there; claiming that they had to look after me to make sure nobody tried to take advantage of me. Tae took me up under his wing. He was teaching me everything that he knew. He liked me; always making sure I ate, asking me if I needed a break, if I was okay. I liked his vibe though. Too bad he worked for Sweets, because I would take him under my pussy wing, but his money wasn't long enough. All Tae did was look out and re-up whenever one of us got low. He was busy though because we were only allowed to have twenty pills at a time, just in case we got caught up.

It was kind of fun ducking the police, hiding in the alleyways and talking in code. I caught on quick. I liked the thrill of out-smarting the police; it gave me a high that I can't explain. I ended up getting some regulars in that short time that came the same time every night looking for me. The fiends were even funny to me; foaming at the mouth and nodding out. A couple of softies wouldn't sell to women that were pregnant and they turned down change. Not me, I counted it all up. If it spends why not take it; and them women were gonna find a way to get high whether we sold to them or not. Now Sweets said it was time to bring me inside so that I could learn the product. *I am gonna miss being out here but I have to keep it moving.*

My downtime consisted of me looking into Diamond and her family affairs. Once I had the information that I was looking for, which just happened to land in my lap. I decided that it would be nice to find the first man in her life, Old Daddy.

His name was Leroy, a boxer that had an incredible opportunity to become a professional, but things went left for him when he got caught up in a domestic abuse case. He knocked Diamond's mother the hell out according to public record. He got arrested and they took his license from him, but come to find out he was training other boxers on the low. From my understanding he was full of wealth, but just like me, Diamond suffered from daddy being missing-in-action. *I have more in common with the girl other than her playing the side chick role to my men. Since she insists on being a part of my juices, it's only fair that I fuck with her DNA. I will have her father giving me all of the unpaid child support that he owes her.*

When I walked into the gym where Leroy was conducting his training all eyes were on me. I was the only female in this musty ass place.

*****

"Hi my name is Leroy, how can I help you?" *In more ways than one.* Diamond had a handsome father. He looked to be about six feet, salt and pepper curly hair, light, clear beautiful eyes; body was banging too. *Oh shit! I could really drop my panties right now; this was one old man that can get it with much pleasure.*

"Hi, I'm Lala," I shook his hand. "I'm looking for a trainer; I was hoping that someone here could help me."

"You're in the wrong place Miss Lady; we only train men in here. I can hook you up with the women's gym, but you don't look like you're a boxer. If you're looking for a fitness gym there are plenty in the area. I can get you a good discount."

"No, I'm in the right place. I came here because I need to be able to protect myself. I'm running from an abusive relationship and I need to know how to fuck him up. A woman can't teach me what a man can!"

"I'm sorry, but you came to the wrong place. We can't help you here; we only train men that are trying to become professional boxers. I'm really sorry that you're in a situation but we don't offer any self-defense classes."

"This is exactly what I need; I'm more than willing to pay," I lied. *This shit better be free.* "Mr. Leroy, if I walk out of here and go home I'm taking a chance of being on the news in the morning. I just need to learn a few techniques, just in case. I'm not leaving here until somebody shows me something. I can't leave here!" I let the fake tears form all in my eyes.

"Okay, I will help you! I don't normally do this but you seem like you're desperate. We can't start until six though, that's when most of the guys will be finished. I can tell you don't want to go home, so I will treat you to a light lunch before we get started. I have to warn you though, fighting is more mental than it is physical. If your mind ain't right, you will lose to him every time."

"That's what I need you for; because my mind ain't right. How much is this going to cost me?"

"Let's just say an old man has empathy for you, so it's free of charge. I can't see myself charging you. I wouldn't want to see a pretty face messed up years down the line." *Just the words I needed to hear from Leroy.*

"Thank you so much. My money is low. Without him taking care of me financially it's been hard to maintain. I woke up this morning to no gas or electric, but I'm a survivor. I'll be okay eventually. He just wants me to run back to him, but not this time. I'll make a way without him."

"Do you have children to take care of?"

"Yes, I have a little boy and a girl. I sent them with my mom for now until I get on my feet." *Old men have always been easy for me to connive; seems like nothing has changed.*

"Don't worry, I'm gonna help you beat him at his own game. Pretty young lady, you and your kids will be just fine. You have a friend in me. He's a coward; I'm tired of these young men doing this to you young girls. You stay right here while I go get my keys. I'll be right back."

I watched him as he walked off and damn did he have a sexy walk. *This old man had some serious swag going on.*

CHAPTER 26

SWIFT
TWO WEEKS LATER

"Shit man, who was it that shot at you?" Moose was vexed.

"I knew this was going to happen; stuff is getting way out of control."

"I don't know who it was. All I know is that I was getting out the car and somebody fired shots. I flew back in the car and laid on the floor. I need you to get me a vest. Somebody tried to take me out!" I was rolling a blunt my nerves were still messed up from the other day.

Jock had just rung the buzzer and was on his way up. He had been consumed with his seed. Nothing much else mattered at the moment.

"What's up?" Jock gave Moose dap and hugged me as if I were already dead in the grave. "I'm glad you're alright. These streets are getting crazier by the minute."

"How's the baby? I'm sorry that I haven't been over there to see him since he came home but uncle been thinking about him. Diamond and I got a bag over there for him, so you can take that home when you leave." I passed the blunt to Moose.

"My little man is fine, nigga. I'm worried about you! It's whatever at this point; somebody tried to take my brother off this earth. What are the plans fellas?" Jock was pacing the floor like he was the one that was shot at. *Now that's some loyalty for your ass.*

"We don't have one yet. We took a vote to strike and I think we struck wrong. I tried to tell y'all that going west wasn't a good idea, but I was out voted. Now we're in a war with Sweets again. We need to call a truce because it's gonna go back and forth."

"Moose is your thinking cap on? Do you hear yourself man? He's down five men right now; he's not looking for a truce. He's looking for blood; it's too late for that! We're in a position now where we have to send some confusion. We need to strike tonight in every direction, even our own." Moose and Jock looked at me like I had lost my mind.

"Are you fucking serious right now? Swift do you hear yourself? You want us to shoot our own. Naw man, I ain't with this shit!" Jock questioned.

"Just hear me out for a minute. If we don't strike at our own then there is no fucking confusion! We need to make it look good; nobody dies they just get a little shot up."

"A little shot up? What the fuck does that mean? Bullets travel, Swift. We can't make no guarantees. Why can't we just strike back? All this other stuff is unnecessary!" Moose wasn't feeling my theory.

"Yeah Swift, I'm with Moose on this one! We never make a hit on our own; the bottom line is, east and west are now beefing. Even if we go at all angles, west will still think that we did the shit anyway. Now we can go thirty to forty deep and fuck some shit up; let them know that we ain't playing no games!"

$$*****$$

Diamond walked in so all conversation came to an end. Not that I don't trust her, she just doesn't need to be involved in everything. The less she knows the better off she is. The meeting was adjourned but I told Jock and Moose that I will hit them up later on.

"Hey, I didn't expect you back so soon."

"I wasn't going too far. Just needed to get a few things from the market. Did I interrupt your meeting with the guys?"

"No, we were just about done anyway." *This chick really loves me. She hasn't left my side since I got shot at the other day.* "I thought you were going to check on your mom?"

"I did that too but she was drunk, as usual, so I just left. Lately I haven't been able to catch her sober. I feel sorry for my little sisters; I don't know how they do it. She gets violent and ignorant."

"Was she always like this?" I can tell by the look on Diamond's face that she's hurting right now.

"My Aunt took me under her wing, so most of the time I wasn't really with her. But even my aunt is worried about her. I don't want to consume you with my problems; you have your own to deal with. I hope Moose and Jock plan on finding out who shot at you and go kill their ass! If I knew who tried you, I would take them out myself!"

"Come here and sit down." I waited for Diamond to sit next to me. "Your problems are my problem. If something is hurting you then it affects me. I want to be a part of all of you. The same way you feel about the bullets that were meant for me, is the same way that I feel about anything that comes your way. We are a team and teams work together. That's the only way that we win. I'm all the way in this. I don't ever want to hear you say anything about your problems consuming me."

"Okay, I hear loud and clearly. What's on your mind Swift? How are you feeling?"

"I'm angry, but I knew it was coming; I just didn't know when. I did a lot of dirt out here in these streets but I humbled myself a little too late. I don't want to beef with nobody. I just want to live my life, enjoy my girl, and have fun. I'm usually the levelheaded one but today I almost caused some major havoc, but my boys hit me with a reality check. I'm going to listen to them because lately I've been making some bad decisions."

"Well how about we just leave, move to another state and start a brand new life. I know you have enough money. This is not gonna go away; I'm afraid of losing you. Every time you walk out that door I drop on my knees and pray to God that you come home safely. The other night was too much for me to handle."

"You pray for me?" *I never had a woman who prayed for me.*

"Yes, I do. I believe in God; he's the creator and he answers prayers. I know the life we lead ain't right, but I ask for his grace and mercy. You have a good heart in there, you just got caught up and it's time to get out. At first it starts out as a money thing, then the power sets in, and next thing you know you're addicted off the high. It's no different than a crackhead or dope feind. Swift, whatever you live by, you die by."

"Diamond, you just said the most realest shit I've ever heard. This is all I know, I don't know how to do anything else. I've been in training since the age of nine. Where would we go? What would I do to feed my high, as you say? My family and friends are here; I just can't up and leave them."

"There's a lot that we can do. You run an illegitimate business; all you have to do is take all that you learned and use that knowledge to run a legal business. As far as your family and friends, I'm sure they would rather see you go then to never be able to see you again. We can't do this anymore. I have family all over, just pick a state and that's where we will land. Or we can travel. There's a whole world out there just waiting on us."

CHAPTER 27

JAY

$\mathcal{T}$hank goodness Boss enrolled the kids in school because at least I had my days to myself. Being a mother was no joke. I had to get up early and get the kids ready for school, make breakfast, lunch, get them on the bus, make sure homework was done and cook dinner. My job seemed like it was never done. This was hard work dealing with three spoiled brats that weren't used to any type of structure. They weren't used to having to listen to authority. Call after call from the school; this one did this, this one did that. It was so exhausting. Then to top it off, Tasha was off living it up, not worried about a damn thing. I think she called once for about five minutes and that was it. *Shoot! She had these kids, not me.* I did have them respecting me a little more. I told Kyle that if he kicked me again I was gonna break both his legs. They were getting there.

Boss had stopped all the partying in the house just like I asked him to, but now him and his entourage were back to renting out hotel rooms. This was something that I was getting tired of.

Did he not realize he had three kids and me to come home to? We barely see him. He would come home in the wee hours of the morning and be back up in the afternoon getting ready to do it all over again. It was getting quite sickening. *I'm too young for this. I should be out living my life. This is not the life that I imagined for myself, especially not in L.A..* Boss and Tasha were not about to turn me into the help. At first when he was in the doghouse he was doing pretty well. As soon as he felt like we were back on good terms, here came the bullshit. I can see that he's the type that needs to stay on the shit list. I shouldn't have to go through all of that to make a man do right. I'm not sure what his idea of fatherhood stands for, but it ain't this. *I need for him to recognize his priorities.*

*****

I'm so happy to be boarding this plane back home. I never thought that I would feel this way. Binky's court date creeped up on me pretty quick. Time flies when you're busy raising kids.

I took the kids to the amusement park for Kyle's birthday. I didn't even know it was his birthday until the day before when Shayla mentioned it. I had to come up with something quick and I put the other two birthdays in my phone. Boss didn't even know when his damn kids were born. Not only was it my first time being at an amusement park; it was theirs too. We got on every ride that we could. Then we came home and had cake and ice cream.

I did manage to get him a couple of gifts, but apparently that's not how their mother did things. All of them got gifts on each other's birthdays. I had to explain to the girls that it wasn't their birthday so they weren't entitled to a gift. Kyle was happy, and that's all that mattered to me. The girls were too whether they wanted to admit it or not. I was thrown into this position and was doing a better job at it than both parents put together.

Tasha did call and wish Kyle a happy birthday and that was it. They were sad that I was leaving. Kyle kept asking me when I was coming back? Why did I have to be gone so long? Was I going to leave them like their mommy did? No matter how much I assured them that I would be back, they didn't believe me. I hated looking at their sad faces.

I wasn't sure that Boss would do what he was supposed to do. I left him a list of things that get done for them on a daily. I had to put in place a backup plan. Tweeny introduced me to this nanny that I could use. She was on standby, just in case I needed her.

Boss has been out of it lately; partying entirely too much. We've been at each other's throats for the last two weeks arguing every day. Hopefully this time away will help our, so-called relationship.

I recently found out that Boss was thirty-eight years old. He got me by thirteen years but he still acts like a kid. *When do men grow the hell up? I can't do this for the rest of my life.*

I'm seriously considering taking Tweeny up on her offer. She was about to go on tour and wanted to take me with her, but I told her that I would let her know because I have these kids to think about. If I can work it out somehow, then I'm going.

I've been working a lot lately; getting booked left and right. I love what I do and the money train was flowing, so no complaints as far as that. I was even able to have the kids on set with me. I would go and get them off the bus and bring them back to work with me. If I didn't do it that way then homework wouldn't get done or nothing else. I'm at work and the kids are calling telling me that they're hungry and that Boss isn't home. I call him up and he tells me he's on his way to the house and two hours later he still hasn't shown up. Then Ashley falls down the stairs; busted her head wide open. I'm at the emergency with her while she's getting her head stitched up and Boss never shows up. After about two times of that back and forth, the only way to make sure they were taken care of was to keep them with me.

*****

The plane landed; back home I was. I caught a cab straight to the projects to go check on Grams. I waved to a couple of people with their nosy asses; they saw everything always in the window. Of course as soon as I opened the door the mice and roaches were running for cover. *Ugh! I can't stand it. I want my grandmother the hell out of here.*

*****

"Hey Grams. How are you?"

Grams was sitting in her rocking chair. She looked up so happy to see me. "Hey Jaylin, it's nice to see you in the flesh."

I gave Grams the tightest hug and kissed her on both cheeks several times. "What's going on?"

"Ain't nothing change, the same old same. I'm just sitting here waiting for the news to come on." Grams was just a rocking away.

"Grams, when are you going to get tired of this life right here? Don't you want to go play bingo or something? You're getting old."

"I am old child." Grams laughed. "This is all I know, Jaylin. I ain't never did much and I don't like going outside no more; it ain't safe. These little yo boys have taken over the community."

"Come with me. I can take care of you. Please Grandma!" She knows that I only call her grandma when I'm pleading with her.

"I've been thinking about it. How is it in Los Angeles? What's it like?"

"I live in the suburbs; it's nice and country like. Sunny and hot; flowers blooming...you can plant a garden in the back yard. You would love it. I can look into some senior programs. No more roaches or mice."

"You always have been scared of rodents, they can't hurt you. I'll think about it. How are those children doing?"

"They're coming along. It's been an adjustment for them and me, but we're getting it together. You can help me with them if you come."

"Yeah, I know. Sounds good, I'm just scared to leave the nest and I don't want to be a burden on nobody. "

"You wouldn't be a burden. You still do everything yourself, just imagine not being a prisoner in your own home. Being able to smell the fresh air. I can see you now in the garden." I was getting excited.

"What about that man of yours? If I come, is he going to be okay with me being there?"

"Grams, he won't care. We have the room for you. The house is huge; it's one of these houses that you see on television."

"When are you going back?"

"It will be sometime next week after Binky's court date. I really could use your help with the kids, that way I could work a little more. You're really going to come back with me?"

"Hey now child, I said I'm thinking about it. Don't go getting your hopes up. Are you staying with me or are you acting brand new again?"

"I already have my hotel room reserved. You just wait Grams, once you get away from here you will see the difference. You've been here so long that you think this is normal living, but it's not."

"Yeah child that's what they all say. Thank you for paying my bills and having Binky's uncle check up on me. He comes by every day, sometimes twice a day."

"Grams, after all that you've done for me that's the least I could do. You know if I have it then I'm going to take care of you."

"Yes I know. You have never been selfish. I remember the days when we didn't have much to eat and you would come back in here with food for me to eat. I don't know what or how you got it and I don't think I want to know, but I ate."

I had to laugh at her. *She's right, she don't want to know all the tricks that I had to pull off in a day just to make sure that she was okay.* I spent the rest of the day just talking and laughing with Grams until it started getting late. Then it was off to the hotel.

*****

Once I was settled in it was time to check on the kids. "Hey Shayla, what y'all doing?"

"Nothing, getting ready for bed. I made sure we all took our baths, homework is done, and I got all our clothes out for tomorrow. I didn't iron them because I know you don't want me messing with that, so I picked out clothes that weren't that wrinkled. Yes, we all brushed our teeth. I made us sandwiches for lunch with fruit and a snack. No, dad is not here, so I'm going to walk us to the bus stop and I won't forget to set the alarm. My key is around my neck."

My eyes were filled with tears. "Thank you Shayla, I didn't know you paid that much attention. Is the alarm on now?"

"Yes, as soon as we walked through the door. You don't have to worry about us. Just make sure you help your friend and grandma."

"I love you Shayla. Thanks again for taking care of your brother and sister. If they get out of line just call me."

"Okay, love you too." Shayla mumbled. "Goodnight."

I hung up the phone relieved. *I want to call Boss, but what's the sense? He didn't even call to see if I made it here safely or not.*

CHAPTER 28

LALA

I just about learned everything that Sweets required of me while I was working on the inside of his drug factory. He finally agreed to do business with me and my money was rolling in.

He would place his order in to his supplier, one of his boys would make the drop to my undercover connection, and that's how Swift was getting his product. It was all working out pretty good and my bank accounts were getting back on track. Little did Swift know, I was still benefiting off of his dollar without getting my hands dirty.

My relationship with Leroy was going good also. Not only was he training me, he was also giving me a good fuck. It was hard luring him right in my pussy. The only problem I was having besides his wife was the fact that he wanted to meet my so-called kids since he was their main provider.

That wife of his was a pain in the ass. Always calling him asking him when he's coming home, where he is. *She get on my nerves.* I told him straight up, tell the bitch don't be interrupting my time. Eventually, I will have to figure out what to do with her. Nobody comes in between my hustle.

*****

"Hello." I was irritated to see that my brother was calling me.

"What's up sis?" Terrance asked.

"Nothing just doing me," I said with an attitude. He hasn't been calling me. The only time I hear from one of them, they need something, and I never come through for them, so why even bother?

"I'm calling you for two reasons. Mom had a heart attack, she's over at Mercy. The doctor's say she's going to be okay. She needs to have some kind of bypass surgery. I figured that I would tell you just in case you wanted to go and visit her."

"Oh no, I'll pass. Only call me about her when she's dead, and I won't be attending the funeral. I would just want to know for my own sanity! Moving right along, what's the other reason?"

"That's how you feel? Really Lala, that's some foul ass shit! You're really one fucked up person. Any normal human would run to their mother's bedside no matter what. Put that shit to the side and go see your mother."

I'm just going to sit right here and act like I don't hear a damn word that he's saying. I'm not going up to any hospital to see that woman.

"You're not going to say anything? Are you there?"

"Yep, I'm here just waiting for you to tell me the other reason you're on my phone." *He's holding me up.*

"I ran into Rock the other day and he told me that you're pregnant. Is that true?"

"Where you see him at? I didn't even know you knew Rock."

"I know Rock; you don't know who I know. What's the deal?"

"If I am, what business is it of yours?"

"Ugh, it's my niece or nephew and you are my sister. That baby doesn't stand a chance with a bitch like you for a mother."

"Listen, you're real funny. I'm hanging up this phone, don't call me anymore wasting my time please. Enjoy your day!"

*****

"Who was that?" Nina asked me. I don't know why she was being so nosy.

"My brother. I need for you to finish what you started. You know Sweets is keeping a tab on that ass. Get to licking!" I laughed but I was so serious. I never had my pussy eaten so well. No man that I have been with compares to Nina. This bitch could get paid by giving lessons to men.

While Nina was handling her business, I had the news on to see my progress staring at me right before Nina gave me the biggest orgasm I've ever had.

Now I'm having another orgasm from watching the condo that Swift called himself taking from me which went up in flames last night. I was waiting on this. I was hoping that they would have showed it last night, but they didn't. *Yay for me! I do wish the whole thing burned down, but the fire department was able to get it under control. Those poor families though, out there screaming for their loved ones. Well, it was only ten people that died; it could have been more.*

The police didn't have any suspects because they had on mask. I did a little stake out, so I knew Swift and Diamond weren't in there when I gave the go ahead to my crackheads. I like working with them…they are cheap. Saved me a lot of money and it was a no hassle deal. I supplied them with enough crack to keep them high for weeks. *That crack shit is amazing; people will do anything and everything for that. Now I have another little hustle to be thankful for. Crack had to be sent from the heavens up above.*

CHAPTER 29

SWIFT

"*D*iamond, I'm telling you she didn't do this! It had to be them uptown boys!" *Diamond was losing it, I need her to keep her cool.* "Calm down! You wanted to move anyway, now we have to move. That's all!"

"Bullshit! Lala had something to do with this; I can feel it in my bones! Uptown didn't do this. They would have made sure that we were in there! The bitch is crazy; she ain't that innocent Lala that you think she is. Now what? Have you talked to Moose and Jock?"

"Jock is not answering. Moose knows what's going on. He's going to Binky's court date today."

"Fuck her! He needs to be worried about us. That fire started in our condo! We got the police all over our asses with no damn alibi. It looks like we had something to do with this! The bitch set us up!"

"I already told you once to calm down. I told Moose not to come. Did you forget that the Red Cross is putting us up for now? If the police are watching us, the last thing we need is for Moose to show up here. Think Diamond!"

"No, you think, Swift! The detective wants to talk to me. What the hell am I going to tell them?"

"Don't be stupid! Tell him that you were with Lexi getting your fucking hair done, and I went to go watch the game at the bar."

"Lexi doesn't do hair; she sells it! I'm going to tell them that I went to buy some hair from my girl. You better hope Lexi holds up her end of the bargain! I've seen her flake before."

"She's getting a couple of stacks. I already spoke to her. Tim is covering for me at the bar. We are good; you just need to make sure that you don't clam up."

"Where are you going?" *Diamond is making this more than it has to be.*

"To give Tim his money and make sure everything went smoothly when the police talked to him."

"Why can't you do that over the phone? I'm not going to feel comfortable with you out here in the streets."

"That's a stupid question…because my phone, as well as yours, could be tapped. I'm not taking any chances, so don't send out no crazy text. Keep your conversations regular. I'm going to be very careful." I walked out of the hotel room. *I hate getting into it with Diamond. We are better than this; we shouldn't even be arguing. Now is the time that we need each more than a little bit.*

Diamond is right we need to get the hell away from here. As soon as this stuff gets straightened out with this fire, we are out. I'm going to talk to Moose and Jock, let them know what's up. Either they can find a replacement for me, or split between the two of them. I'm tired of this beef with Sweets; I know the Uptown boys have it in for me, if they haven't already tried. Too many close to death situations in a short period of time. I'm not trying to be dead or laid up in somebody's hospital. If I find out that Lala had anything to do with this fire, she's a dead bitch! I'm going to personally let Diamond handle her and get her satisfaction, then I'm putting a bullet in her head to end her miserable ass life. I put that on my dick.

CHAPTER 30

JAY

*T*he lawyer that Boss got for Binky delivered. We were waiting for Bink to come up the stairs. She was being released on house arrest for the first three months, then she could look for a job during the day and had to be in by eight every night.

Once she secured a job then she could come off the bracelet for good. So far, today was a good day. I had just hung up the phone with Binks' uncle, letting him know the deal, when Moose came strolling down the hallway.

*****

"Aww shoot, she's smiling! You happy your girl is coming home?" Moose was grinning from ear to ear.

"And you know it. Thanks Moose, for riding this ride with Binky." I gave Moose a hug. "I didn't know you cared like that."

"I got mad love for the Bink. She would have done it for me. I'm just not that dude to really settle down. I just have limits when it comes down to you women. I notice the change in her since she came back from L.A. though, but it's all good."

"All you have to do is fight for her, if you want her."

"Naw, I'm not no 'do right' type of dude. If she has to move on to find happiness then let her go ahead. She's going to always be my boo though. Have you seen the news since you've been back?"

"No, why?"

"The condo that Swift was living in burned down. The fire started in his place but ten other people ended up getting burned the hell up. Swift and Diamond had just left. We ain't sure who did what, but it had to be an attack on them. My gut is telling me that your old girlfriend had something to do with it. Swift is thinking that the uptown niggas had something to do with it, but that's not how they roll. Hustlers don't think about no shit like that unless them knockers are planning on running up in the house and stuff has to be disposed of. Dudes are just straight up when they come for you; it ain't no guessing game. They want you to know that it was them. She's doing shit and ain't thinking about the consequences that come along with it, if you know what I'm saying."

I knew exactly what Moose was saying. Lala was basically part of *The Walking Dead;* soon to see the ground. "Wow! I don't know her anymore, and I haven't had any contact with her in a while."

"Greed, she wants that money. See I'm stingy not greedy. Swift showed her life now she doesn't know what to do without it; that's all I can think of. Diamond's on a hunt for her also. She fucked up the Bentley a couple of times. Even if you do see her, stay the hell away before you get caught up in the wrong place at the wrong time type of thing."

I nodded in agreement. Lala was the last person that I wanted to see but if I did happen to run into her; I'm whooping that ass on the strength of Binky. I might even catch up with Diamond to see what trouble we can cause together. Diamond never did anything to me; as far as I was concerned, we were cool. "Well she's making a nice little coffin for herself. I hope she enjoys the hell that she's going to. I had a lot of love for La, you know how close we were, but what she did to Bink really showed me that she don't give a damn about nobody but herself."

*****

"Here she comes, the Bink" Moose was just as excited as me. He didn't smile much but he was smiling today.

"Oh yeah!" I was excited.

Binky ran over to Moose and me. Group hug was in motion while Binky and I wiped the tears from our eyes.

"Stop it you two, I ain't having none of this. Dry up them tears, the girl is home now! Let's make it do what it do! Jay, how did you get here?" Moose replied.

"I caught a cab."

"Alright I'm going to drop you two off at Binks'. I know the clock is ticking for her. Then I'll run to the sub shop, snatch up some food and get us some drinks." Moose said.

"That sounds good." *The projects were going to feel like heaven to her compared to that hellhole.* "I just need to get my stuff from lock-up. I have an hour." Binky said.

"Man, fuck that stuff! Let them have it!" Moose was serious.

"My phone, ID and clothes are in there. I have to get it Moose." Binky replied.

"Okay, come on. Let's go." Moose said as the three of them walked out the courtroom to go to his car.

The whole ride the three of us chatted it up reminiscing on the good times. While Binky was in lock-up getting her belongings, Moose and me stayed in the car waiting on her.

"Jay, I'm serious about your girl. Stay away from her. I don't want you getting caught up in her mess." Moose called himself warning me once again.

"I'm not. Trust me, she's not even trying to be around me."

"Here comes Binky. That was quick." I noticed Moose was looking every which way to make sure he had his back covered. No telling what was going on with him and these streets, but I was happy when he dropped us both off at Binky's, assuring that Bink didn't go over her hour of allowed time.

*****

"Home sweet home. Hey Unc, did you miss me?" Binky asked.

"Sure did. I'm glad to see you." He kissed Bink on her forehead.

"So fill me in, what did I miss?" Bink asked me.

I filled Binky in on what's been going on with Boss, the kids, and me. I told her a little bit about Lala.

"You look like you feel bad for her. I don't, these past four months have been hell. Look at my knuckles. It's not a nice sight. I had to fight damn near every day that I was in there. A couple of times I got my ass whooped by some big ass manly looking chicks. They respected me though because I wasn't backing down. I wasn't gonna let them turn me out no licky licky over here. Lala's jealous ass didn't have to turn me in. I don't have any love for her at all. I'm actually looking forward to her funeral. Every bitch has to have their day, and it looks like hers is coming. Every charge I got was behind her ass and she turns around and does this?" Bink was taking out her braids. "Damn, my hair grew."

"Yes it did." I was admiring Binky's length; she always had long hair anyway. "I don't feel bad for her, she dug this grave."

"Yep, she's cold-hearted. Lala was doing a little more than you think to get a dollar. I caught her a couple of times messing around with them old men. Always around the first of the month. Why you think they were looking for her? Swearing up and down she wasn't doing nothing for them. She knows how to use her body to get what she wants; even back then she was always up to no good. She's been treating us differently ever since we broke all of her commandments. Remember how bad she went off? She tripped me out running around here acting like she was some kind of god. Then she was trying to pimp us. Talking about we owed her because she turned us on. Bitch please, I fucked for mine."

"Yeah, I remember when she pulled that stunt." I laughed. "She had her hand out and everything asking where was her cut? We both looked at each other like 'a cut of what.'"

*****

Moose came through the door with food and drinks. Binks' uncle was glad to let him in. The food and drinks did it because he was funny acting. Bink ate her sub, all the fries and some wings. We didn't know when she was going to stop eating.

"Sorry y'all, but that food in there was horrible. I couldn't wait to get home to eat. Y'all see how much weight I lost. Now I can't wait to get into that water; a shower that I'm going to be in for a long while. But I'll wait on that since I have company."

"Don't let us stop you, go clean that thang up girl!" Moose said.

Binky and I laughed so hard.

"I'm texting Jock and telling him to come through. Nevermind Jay, you text him. Tell him to come have a drink with us and to bring a blunt." Moose said.

"He hit me right back, he's on his way. Party over here, just like old times!"

"I wish you could stay, but I know you have to go back. Don't leave me, Jay." Binky was shaking me in a joking way.

"I'll never leave you, Bink, I'll always be here for you. I'm team Binky!" I yelled.

"I don't know if y'all should have a drink, y'all already sentimental. The liquor is gonna have you two crying and shit." Moose laughed; he was enjoying himself.

*****

Jock showed up while Binky was in the shower with some more food and drinks; as if we weren't full enough. She was in there, no lie, had to be a good hour. We had a field day with that. Uncle was banging on the door like he had to pay the water bill. We all fell out laughing when Binky yelled, "It's free, it's free!" Even Uncle had to laugh at himself. What he meant to say was that he had to use the bathroom. Not even two minutes later he went and took a piss stroll, as we called it.

We tried waiting on Binky, but she was taking too long, so we got started with the drinks. By the time she decided to join us we were already tipsy. We were up to the wee hours of the morning drunk talking, until one by one we all fell asleep in Binks room. What a wonderful time we had with our ex-boos. One thing we will never be able to say about Jock and Moose was that they didn't know how to have fun. We could always let our hair down and they could always loosen up the belt.

Binky was the first to wake up, still on that jail time. Pinching me and laughing, shit wasn't funny. My head was banging. Hung the hell over is what I was. It didn't help that the four of us was crunched up in a full size bed. I couldn't do anything but laugh. Jock heard me, so he looked up at me and smiled. I expected him to jump up and run home to his baby mama, but he didn't. He acted like he didn't have a care in the world. Moose was knocked out, so Binky went and got some ice and put in down his pants. We counted to three and sure enough he jumped up ready to swing, until he realized where he was. "What the fuck?"

Moose went to the bathroom and came back smiling with Ciroc in one hand, pineapple in the other; ready for round two. Just when I was about to ask about eating breakfast Uncle peaked his head in the room, talking about he was about to start cooking since we were up. *Back at it again! Yep, we did it all over again.*

CHAPTER 31

LALA

"Lala, I told you last week that I wanted to see you!" Rock was yelling in my ear. "How are you and that baby coming along?"

"I know Rock, I'm sick all the time. Half the time I don't want to get up. Please stop yelling at me, my head is hurting. Please tell me why Swift is still alive? I been watching the news just like you said, and nothing has happened."

"Listen baby girl, you can't rush perfection! It will be done before he finds out, just continue to lay low." Rock assured.

"Pregnant women don't have patience, Rock. Tiz didn't get kilt on perfection. He was killed out of emotions. How do you know my brother, Terrance? I didn't want my family in my business."

"Oh, me and T go way back. He works for me every now and then when things get rough. He's a good guy; I like your brother a lot."

"Yeah, well I don't! Please don't tell him my business!" La demanded.

"I got you. Well, I want to be at that next doctor's appointment! If you're sick all the time then the baby probably ain't doing too good." *I just might have to put Rock on the hit list if he don't calm down about this fake ass baby. He's starting to be a problem for me.*

"The baby is fine; it's me that's not. We're not sure if this baby is related to you or not. I don't think you need to be getting attached." La said nervously.

"I know, but I'm leaning more towards that it is. You two were getting it in. I heard my cousin fucking your brains out. I used to listen to y'all all the time. You know I had them keys, just in case of an emergency. Yeah boy, my cousin was stroking." *Did this motherfucker just laugh like the shit was funny?* Rock said bragging like it was a family trait.

"Hmm you just made me sick, Rock!" I hung up the phone on that sick bastard. *If Tiz were alive I would smack him from here to the North Pole. I haven't heard from Leroy all day. Let me give my old boo a call and see what he's up to.*

*****

"Hey beautiful, I'm kind of tied up at the moment." Leroy was whispering to me.

"What the fuck she got you doing now?" I asked.

"We're at a banquet for our daughter. I told you this was going to be a rough week for me." I can't help but to roll my eyes. It's a commandment of mine to never be second. As long as he was making me first we were okay, but now I'm starting to feel like a side chick. *Ain't no way.* Even though there are special circumstances to his reason for being in my life, but still, certain shit I just don't put up with.

"Are you coming when it's over?" I asked.

"No, I won't see you all week. I'm on vacation from the gym; she has a lot planned for us this week. Baby, I'm sorry but I will make it up to you. I have to go now." *Oh yeah he's gonna regret that shit, and he will be seeing me this week.* If I have to go knock on the front door then that's what I will do. My mother should have asked me how to get my father. She would have had my father by now. *She never wanted to listen to me.*

Who do these people think I am? Why do they want to play with the La? Don't they know that I invented the word called 'game?' I can't be beat at this. I really just need some head right now, but Nina's dumb ass can't get away from Ugh Mug Sweets. I'll be glad when all of this is over. It's gonna be Lala's world!

*****

What does Terrence want now? I asked him not to call me no more. That woman must be dead. "What is it now? Did she die?"

"You don't even sound like you care at all. Whatever happened to answering the phone with a 'Hello?' No, she's not dead! But I could have been. Your ex came looking for you today. He put a gun to my head!"

"My ex? Who?"

"Swift. You know who I'm talking about." *Actually I didn't. Who does Terrance think he yelling at?* "I have kids to take care of, kids that I need to be around for."

"Terrance, you're still here. Everybody has to die one day, and you're still gonna have kids. What was his reason?"

"You, you were his reason! He's looking for your dumb ass! Thank God he believed me when I told him that I didn't know where you were."

Soft ass Swift; a real gangster would have taken old bro out. "I'll handle it. Get yourself together. Did you call the police?"

"No, you get yourself together. You can't hide out forever! No, I didn't involve the police. I'm not trying to end my life sooner than it has to be. I'm just glad it was me and not mom." Terrance said like it was a relief. *I wish it was her. That would have taken her out for sure, especially since she already has a bad heart.*

"I would have loved to see that!"

"You sick bitch!" Terrance hung up the phone.

Yes, that would be me Bro. One day you're going to learn to stop hanging up on me. Let me give Swift a call and find out what his point was.

*****

"Yeah," Swift answered.

"Was that supposed to scare me? It didn't just to let you know. I don't know why you would put my punk ass brother into this. He can't handle stuff like this, but you can do me a favor. Go find my father and mother...blow their brains out. Next time, just call me. You know my number."

"You got some serious issues. What do you care about?"

"Ummm, let me see what does Lala care about? Oh, I know the answer...MONEY! Makes the world go around. I can rule the world if I have enough of it."

"That can't be it because I have never known you to work. When you work, it generates money; this thing that you care about. It has to be something else."

"Power of the pussy. Yeah, I like the sound of that." I was bopping my head like it was a rap song.

"Yeah, that would sound good to you; it gets used up a lot. I can't believe I fucked with a dummy like you."

"Oh, but you were loving the dummy and I got paid for you to love me, but I'm the dumb one? That math don't add up, Boo. What do you want with me anyway?"

"You tried to play the hell out of me. I knew that Diamond would seal the deal and have your ass pissed off. I don't believe in being mad by myself. You got me fucked up so I had to fuck you better."

"I'm still playing you, and you're still paying me…little do you know." *Swift is interrupting me from admiring myself in the mirror.*

"What is that supposed to mean? You wish I would give you another dime. You're at your last train stop. You fucked up the Bentley, not once, but twice. I let you have that. I can't give you this one; I made a promise on my dick."

"Oh, I wouldn't do that if I were you. So, you made a little promise? Because that's not a big promise for you to make."

"I can't wait to just shut that mouth up for good."

"You are running around handing out death threats like I give a fuck about dying. If I die then it's just my time to go. From what I hear, your ass has dodged several bullets, but the right one will hit you really soon."

"Oh bitch, you care, because if you didn't you would walk around freely. So death does have you shook. Please don't insult my street knowledge. When a nigga don't care about life or death he shows you that. Don't count the bullets that I've dodged, I got one that's headed straight for your temple."

"I'm not hiding; I've been out and about! Lala hides from no man or woman. Matter of fact, where is your bitch? Inquiring minds want to know!" *I'm gonna make Swift wish he never messed with me.*

"I think Diamond is out looking for you as we speak, but it doesn't matter, one of us will catch up to you!" Swift said with confidence.

"You took your head out of that raunchy ass pussy for her to go find me? Wrong move, Boo." Lala laughed.

"Raunchy? I know you ain't talking; as many dicks as you have stroked, sucked, and fucked. Before I got with you and cleaned you up, your shit was like Mississippi burning. I don't ever remember hearing nothing like that about Diamond."

"Yep, burning…just like that condo of mine. The one you stole from me. Where are y'all staying at by the way?" *Swift wants to throw digs; I'm throwing the ball where it hurts down to the bottom of his gut.*

" I underestimated you just a little bit. Peoples loved ones died in that fire." Swift said.

"Peoples loved ones died out here in these streets on the account of you and your trigger happy self. Don't come at me like you so sentimental about the human life." Lala replied.

"Do me a favor, because I'm going to stop playing games with you. Look out the window of that condo you own. I'm parked right next to this black BMW. By the way, it's quite nice. How long did you think it would take me before I would find you?" Swift asked.

I ran to the window and looked down in the parking lot. Swift was sitting on the hood of his car.

"Yep, it's me; cat got your tongue now? Show me how fearless you are. Come on out here and play, Boo Boo." Swift laughed. "I got that ass now."

CHAPTER 32

JAY

*T*oday was a very sad day and my emotions were all over the place. Just last week we were partying like rock stars. Now today, it was time to say goodbye. *I don't know if I can do this. I'm really not built for these funerals. I always fall apart.*

I can't believe that somebody cut Jocks head off and left it on the hood of Swift's car. Anything is possible in B-more, but this shit right here was wicked. It's like my whole life stopped. Not a day went by that I wasn't crying.

I was supposed to have been back in a L.A. but then this happened, forcing me to stay longer. To make matters worse, it ain't easy watching two thugged out dudes lose their cool to the point where they can't even function. All we had were each other; the same pain that we shared was all understood. None of us could hold each other up; we were all falling. This nagging feeling in my heart just wouldn't let up or leave me. I prayed to God for help to take this pain away, which is something that I rarely do. I wake up thinking about Jock and what little sleep that I was getting he was all that I was dreaming about. Grams was trying her hardest, but even she didn't know what to do to help me. She just kept saying that it's a process that we all have to go through.

Binky being on house arrest, she couldn't even attend the funeral. I have to do this all on my own. *I can't wait to get this over with and get far away from here.* This was war. Swift and Moose had no intentions on letting this slide. Nobody even knew how this happened to him. All we know is that his car ended up being parked right in front of his house, but his baby momma said she never saw Jock. We know that it didn't happen there; whoever did it parked his car there. None of the neighbors saw anything. The police really had nothing to go on. The streets were quiet, so it's a long shot even trying to figure out who did this to him. Swift and Moose were becoming reckless. Every day somebody was turning up dead.

*****

Boss was working my nerves. He kept asking me over and over when I was coming back. Which I don't know why, when I'm there he doesn't spend any time with me. He was still doing the same thing. Every time I spoke to him he was partying it up, doing his usual. Me being there wouldn't make a difference at all. I guess he would feel comfortable knowing where I was.

I still managed to talk to the kids but even they missed me and were losing hope of me returning. They still hadn't heard from Tasha, and Shayla said she saw her father more when I was there. Boss was really showing his entire ass. I was tempted to call that nanny that Tweeny introduced me to so that Shayla could get a break from playing the parenting role. *She needs to be able to be a kid and not grow up so fast.* As soon as I was going to, Moose made the arrangements.

Jocks father didn't have insurance nor did nobody else in his family. I helped him out by paying for all the flower arrangements and the food for the repass. I'm having it catered. I didn't want to put that burden on the family to cook the food. But I'm determined that after this funeral, I'm saying my goodbyes to Binky, then me and Grams are getting on the plane. I have no reason to return either. When Binky gets off house arrest she can come visit me. I'm done with this city. I can't take any more of this. *Let me call Bink and see how she's over there making out.*

*****

"Hey girl," Binky answered.

"Hey, I'm getting ready to slip on my black dress." I was tearing up.

"I know, everybody is out here getting in their cars. I'm just staring out the window. It looks like the funeral home is going to be packed. I feel so bad that I can't be there with you. I can't even say goodbye. I tried to see if the judge would let me out to go, but he said it's not my immediate family. If he only knew. What family do I have? I don't even know my family but I knew him."

"I know, Bink. That's just how the system works. It's messed up. Just be glad that you were home in time to spend some time with him before he was taken away. We laughed until the sun came up. Who knew that when he left out that morning that would be the last time we would see him. This is so messed up. One minute I'm angry; the next minute I'm hurt. I just don't know if I'm coming or going." I reached to grab some more tissue to wipe my eyes. "Damn, I just finished beating my face. I should have put on that waterproof makeup. I don't know what I was thinking."

"I know none of us are in our rights minds. Poor Swift. That was a message to him. Can you imagine the guilt he must be feeling right now? I don't think he will ever be the same again; seeing Jock's head on that hood. If he ever finds out who did this, he's going to take out the whole family and anybody associated to them."

"I just know how I feel, so for Swift it has to be twenty times worse, and I'm not coping with this pain too well."

"How are you getting there? Do you think you will be okay to drive?" Binky was concerned about me.

"I rented a car. I'm not depending on nobody to bring me back. I'm only staying at the repass for a little while, and then I'm out. I can't be bothered with the spectators." I slipped on my dress.

"Well you go ahead. Bring me back a flower please." Binky hung up the phone on me, crying.

*****

I finished getting dressed and headed over to the funeral home. The line was out the door and around the corner. Cars were everywhere. People respected Jock, he had a lot of associates and he knew a lot of people. I ended up parking the rental like three blocks away and walked my way back down. The closer I got the more reality was sinking in.

I saw Swift and Moose; they were close to the front of the line. Moose pulled me up with them and whispered in my ear "You're family, you go in with us." I gave them both a tight hug as the funeral director opened the doors to start letting the people in.

As soon as I looked at the infant in front of us I knew that had to be Jock's baby. He looked just like him. What I didn't expect was for Tracey to be his baby momma. There's no way she didn't know about me when she used to live two courts down from me. *Sneaky, trifling bitch.* I took my focus off her as we were getting closer to the casket.

I could hear the people in the back, sniffles and moans, all the Oh my God's. In front of us must have been his father, who wasn't taking it too well at all. I never had the opportunity of meeting him. Jock had four other brothers that he didn't mess with; too tough. I'm guessing that was who was holding up Jock's father. I was looking around to see if I could point out his mother, but I didn't see her. I never met her either. A couple of his cousins that I knew were up there also, not doing too well.

Now it was our turn to go up. It was a closed casket. I had Moose on one side and Jock on the other. All three of us were dressed in all black with our shades on. I had to be the strong one for them because they were both broke down. Somebody from the back came up and helped me get them seated. I don't even know who it was. I just mumbled 'thank you.'

The funeral was so packed that people were left standing on the outside waiting to get in to pay their respects. Just about every drug boy from the east side was there. Some I recognized and some I didn't. It was too many to know them all. There wasn't a dry eye in sight.

The funeral was long; everybody had something to say or a story tell about Jock. I was rubbing Swift's back to try and comfort him in some way. *I know I saw Diamond come through that line.* I was wondering why she wasn't over here with her man, but as I glanced back to where the screaming was coming from, Lexi was carrying her out. *She couldn't help Swift.*

Moose was trying to hold it together until it was time to leave and go to the gravesite. That's when anger set in for him and he just started swinging his fist in the air with his legs trembling. He stood up and started screaming from the top of his lungs, "SOMEBODY KILLED MY BROTHER! JOCK YOU BETTER BE HITTING ME UP LATER. YOU DIDN'T GO OUT LIKE THIS MAN! JOCK! JOCK! JOCK!"

Swift and I knew that we had to get him out of here, so we missed the final prayer. Once we got him outside I knew that neither one of them were in no shape to drive. I told Swift that I would go get my rental and that they were riding with me. He didn't even put up a fuss; I guess he knew. I went, got the car and double-parked in the street, and I waved to both of them to get in here with me. As soon as they got in, people that were inside of the funeral home started coming out. It took a while for everyone to get out and head to their cars.

One of Jock's workers was punching the brick on the funeral home and busted all ten of his knuckles; blood was pouring out. Moose was still in the back sniffling and Swift was wearing a big sign on his face that read 'DANGER.' The whole ride to the cemetery was dead silence.

*****

We got out the car, huddled around the casket and let the funeral director complete the service. I grabbed three flowers, one for Grams, Binky, and me. We walked back to the car and headed to the repass, which was only across the street from the funeral home. Calmness came over me because it was over. Jock was at his final resting place and soon I would be going home.

When we got to the repass I could tell there was a little bit of tension going on towards Swift. Jock's brothers must have blamed Swift for his death because they gave Moose daps and acted like Swift wasn't there.

Diamond and Lexi came and sat at the table with us. We all had plates of food, but no appetite. It was getting close to the time for me to leave. *I want out of here.* So many people coming up to the table to hug us saying, 'I'm sorry for your loss.' *One more of those and I just might explode.* Poor Tracey was sitting at the table looking lonely, not too many people coming up to her. The baby was being tossed around from table to table.

*****

It was time for me to make my exit so I gave everyone a hug at the table, told Moose and Swift to text me when they made it home safely and bounced. As soon as I made it to my car I heard a very familiar voice calling my name.

"Jay! Jay!"

"Yes, Lala," I questioned. *Why are you even anyplace near here?*

"How was it?" Lala asked. "Sorry I didn't make it. I know the kind of pain you're in; remember I just went through it with Tiz."

She's in all black with a black cap trying to cover her face. I can't believe her; she didn't care nothing about Tiz.

"It was terrible." I said as I unlocked my door.

"Wait Jay, where are you going?"

Why is she questioning me like we are friends? If I wasn't so drained from this funeral I would be wailing on that ass. "Get the fuck away from me Lala!"

"Wait! Don't leave. I have a proposition for you that you can't refuse." Lala said with enthusiasm in her voice. *Like I was supposed to be jumping for joy.*

"Girl please, I don't have time for any of your get rich schemes and now is not even an appropriate time to be talking about this nonsense! You need to get the hell out of here before you find yourself at your own funeral." I knew that if Swift or Moose saw her some shit was gonna pop off.

"You won't need Boss-man. You will have your own money. I can teach you the ropes."

"No thank you, but thanks for the offer." I was being sarcastic. "Your type of hustling will get a bitch killed." I jumped in the car, went straight to Binky's to say my goodbyes and give her the obituary and flower that I got for her.

*****

Binky must have seen me when I pulled up because she had the door open standing there waiting for me to come in. I held it in as long as possible. As soon as Binky saw me she hugged me and wouldn't let me go. I finally broke down after such an emotional day. Uncle even held me for a long time so that Binky could get herself together. Once I calmed down I filled Binky and Uncle in on the details of what happened at the funeral. *Here we go again crying.* Even Uncle was shedding tears. I wanted to hold out on Binky about Lala but I had to get it off my brain, it was tearing me up inside. I made the mistake of telling Binky about the whole situation with La being outside the repass.

"La had the nerve to be outside of the repass hiding like the chicken bitch that she is. Oh yeah, she's a special kind of crazy, but

I'm on another level of crazy that she ain't never seen before. I'm telling you now that she better be glad I'm on lockdown! Why the fuck didn't you pick up something and hit the bitch? She's so damn disrespectful; coming at you on some hustling shit when Jock still sitting on the top of his grave. You're grieving and she comparing her and Tiz! I'm sick to my stomach about this!" Binky got up and walked in the kitchen to pour herself a stiff one. "Jock bought this for us, I told him I was saving it for the next go round, remember? He waved his hand around and said 'Don't worry about it, drink it up.'"

I should have just kept my mouth closed. I know how Binky can fly off the handle real quickly. When she gets angry and hurt she doesn't think; she acts. Now I'm torn, do I get on that plane or not? "Binky calm down, you have to stay focused. When this is all said and done." I pointed at her bracelet. "You're coming to L.A. with me. I should be more established and you're going to do hair. Not just any around the way girls, I'm talking a celebrity stylist. We're gonna be two little girls that grew up in this murder capital and made it out! I need you to see this vision and believe in it. If I have to call you every five minutes and speak these same words then I will."

"What vision Jay? I can't see past the next hour. Jock was just here, and now he's gone. We weren't your typical little girls, Jay. When the girls were playing with Barbie's and dreaming of having a husband and kids, we were sneaking and watching porn so we could learn how to suck dick for a living. We were trying to learn how to lie on our backs and grind from the bottom. We used to steal Barbie heads so that I could learn how to do hair and you could learn how to do make-up. We were the best little thieves before we even had a damn nipple. We knew how to insert a tampon before we even had a damn period! We were jerking niggas off as a test run before they even reached puberty! We were fast little girls that no mother wanted their little girls around. Neither one of us had a mother to raise, teach, and train us. So we latched on to Lala and let her reel us right in, just like she had been doing. Have you ever asked yourself why Lala doesn't have any skills besides sucking and fucking? I'll answer; she never got her hands dirty. She always told us to do it while she watched and directed!"

"Binky we've grown so much. Just like you said, we had very little direction. But it's okay; we are better women today than we've ever been. We've lived a little and grown a lot. We're not still stuck. This vision I have for us is real and it's a legal one. It's a job doing something that we are thorough at. When I get back I'm going to sign up for school so that I can get my certification. When you come to L.A. you're going to get your beauticians license while working. We're going to be busy doing positive things. I'm going to set you up before you even get there. I'm making some good connections; I can start showcasing your talent while I'm out there. I'm not gonna set us up for failure."

"We thought we were out this hood before, everything looked promising and we ended up right back. We already did this, Jay. The only difference is it's just thousands of miles with a different hustle. What's your back up plan if one of them celebrities on the rise get mad at you for some reason and black ball you throughout the whole industry? What's your plan if stuff doesn't work out between you and Boss-man? I mean the relationship is already on the rocks!"

"The way I see it is we can keep staying stuck in the same position or we can choose to do better. Do you want to stay on the bottom or try to reach the top? I'm taking all this negative energy back with me to L.A. and turning it into a positive. I have nothing to lose, but everything to gain, so while the situation presents itself I'm going to take full advantage of it. I'm looking to be a better me. No, I don't have a backup plan right now, but I'm going to get one. As far as me and Boss-man, if it doesn't work out then so be it. I'll tell you what…we won't be back here. Change your mindset Binky; it's up to you. I'm getting ready to go over to the next court and gather up Grams so we can head to the airport. I want to know before I leave here, are you with me or not?"

"Okay, I'm with you. I just don't want to be disappointed." Binky gave me a hug goodbye.

"Life is full of disappointments, it's just how you deal with it, sis. I love you and will call you when we land." I knew that Uncle was somewhere in there listening to every word with his nosey self. "Hey Uncle, we're taking you with us too. I know you're listening." I walked out on my way to my next journey in life.

CHAPTER 33

SWIFT

"*D*iamond, we must have looked at over fifty places in the past two weeks; I need you to choose one. Our time is running out here and I want to be gone. What's it going to be?" I was asking Diamond because I refused to go look at another place. We had looked at houses to buy, condominiums, apartments, row houses, you name it we looked at it and she still didn't pick one. Even the realtor was getting impatient.

Diamond was watching her soap opera's trying to ignore me so I took the remote and turned the television off. "I haven't picked one because I don't plan on staying here. I'm not going to sit around here and wait for someone to kill you."

"What? We've already had this conversation over and over again. We are leaving, just not right now. I can't leave Moose and I have to find out who did this to Jock. What happened to my ride or die chick?"

"She decided to live, and realized that her life was important. When a niggas head got chopped off that's when I hop off at this stop. It's too much for me to handle. I've been in the drug game; I can handle that, but all this other stuff…this I don't want any part of. It's out of my league. You found Jock's head on top of your hood and you still want to stay here? Do you think I want to walk outside and see your head on the car? Fuck B-more, let's go or I'll go by myself! Every little sound and you're up grabbing that damn gun. Don't you want some peace?"

"You're really going to leave me here, Diamond?" *I hear her loud and clear but I can't leave just yet.*

"What I'm saying is that you're getting sloppy with your dealings. Trying to set a trend like it's the latest fashion. Shooting up everyone in sight, it's only a matter of time before shit hits home again. I don't want my family to come outside and find my head sitting on their damn porch! I don't want to be sitting at another motherfucking funeral of someone that I care about!"

"Yo, you tripping! You be watching the news too much. What trend am I setting? I'm trying to get niggas to talk."

"No I'm watching, Swift! Did that bitch ever tell you that you talk in your sleep? Did she ever tell you that you have nightmares?"

"Yo, what the fuck you talking about? You know that I don't deal with riddles, just tell me straight up! Sitting on shit gets you shitted on!" *I'm so hurt right now but I have to be a man about it and stand my ground.*

"You come in at night and tell on yourself in your sleep. Everything you did comes out your mouth. That's probably how she found out about us. I know more than you think I do."

"I'm going to tell you like I told her, when I'm talking in my sleep I'm dreaming about things that I want to do. You can't take that stuff serious. You're blowing all of this out of proportion. You wanting to part ways could be saying that you found somebody else and are using this as an excuse." I was trying to change the subject and put Diamond on a guilt trip.

"Did you even hear what I just said? This has nothing to do with me finding somebody else; this is about my life being at stake. It's time that I start doing things differently."

"This is some bullshit! I just lost my boy and now my girl too. You are trying to kick me when I'm down."

"No, I'm not! It didn't make sense for you to spend money and get a place of my choice when I know that I'm not going to be there. You can have the Bentley back; I'm going to get me a one way train ticket to some place far away from here."

"So you have this all thought out? I see how it is now. Well, Swift won't be begging a chick to stay with him. You better be sure that this is what you want because ain't no coming back."

"I'm not asking you to beg. I'm asking you to come with me on that train. Swift, I love you, if I didn't, we wouldn't even be having this conversation."

"I need a little more time, that's all I'm asking."

"A little more time doesn't consist of you signing a lease for six months to a year. I gave you enough time. I'm getting on that train today."

"Today? Just like that? What time?" *I can't believe she's throwing this on me so last minute. There's no way I even have time to set up a move like this.*

"The train leaves at four and I'm going to be on it." *I can't stand seeing Diamond cry like this.*

"I can't leave today, but I can meet you. Just give me a week." *I'm giving myself seven days to get everything in order so that I can leave. Diamond is my world.*

"My first stop will be North Carolina; I plan on staying there for about a week. Then I will be off again, I'm not sure where yet. I have some family that I'm going to visit there."

"Okay, just give me a week baby, and I'll be there." *All bets are off. Whatever don't get done just won't get done. I have seven days to find out who put Jocks head on the hood of my car.*

CHAPTER 34

JAY

I came home to the kids that really missed me dearly. It was nice to feel the warmth and knowing that someone missed me. They filled me in with all that I missed out on, showed me their homework, upcoming school projects, and papers that needed to be signed for school field trips. Kyle wanted to run track and needed parental consent that Boss could have signed, but he didn't. I got them settled and back on track because they were a little off schedule, but Shayla did the best that she could do. *I'm so proud of her.*

The kids were enjoying Grams, she was teaching them how to cook, clean, and do their laundry. Grams said we were raising self-sufficient kids. Real funny because she never taught me how to cook until I moved here and all those frequent calls helped me. The kids were even learning how to plant in the small garden that she started. It brought chills all through my body to see my Grams dream of having her own garden come true. I know I was getting spoiled.

Grams was nothing but a blessing; I didn't have to worry about the kids, so I was picking up extra gigs. I even enrolled myself into school but I had at least a couple of months before I started. *Getting paid, getting paid, I'm saving up for when Binky comes.* I was sending her money, making sure that she and Uncle was alright. So far; so good. She had her head on straight.

*****

I was so busy; Jock crossed my mind but mainly at night when I went to bed. The pain was starting to ease. I gave Grams his obituary and as she was reading it she threw it back at me. She told me that for years there had been speculation that his dad killed my mom. She knew that I was messing with Jock but never knew who his father was. As soon as she saw his birth name that's when it clicked in her head. I hit a sour spot in her heart; I think that if she would have read it before we got on the plane that she wouldn't have come with me. By the time we landed and she felt the warm breeze of L.A. she was back to her normal self.

I wonder if he knew and if that's why he never really brought me around his family. Had I known I don't think that I could have been with Jock. If that was true, then his father took a part of me that I would never be able to experience. It still didn't change the love that I had for Jock. I did notice though that Grams hadn't been asking me how I was feeling, lately. She probably felt relieved that Jock's father had to experience the pain that she felt.

*****

On the flip side, Boss has been foaming at the mouth, and I'm no dummy. He's not just drinking, dipping and dabbing; he's a full fledge addict. Some days he's nodding like they do at the Lexington Market. He has that lean where I think he's going to fall but never hits the floor because he jumps back up. Other days he's speed racing, chasing, and hearing things that are not there. *This has been going on for some time. That explains the late nights and sleeping all day.*

His appearance was going down just as fast as his bank account. Bills were coming in unpaid and the bill collectors were calling the phone. He was losing his artists left and right; his reputation was on the line. His credibility was at an all time low and most importantly, the kids noticed. Grams hadn't said anything yet because she was waiting on me to start that conversation. Since I was working more in the industry the more I was hearing and none of it was good.

Tweeny said the last track that Boss produced for her was garbage. She moved on to another producer and her rap song was doing well on the radio. Moose, Jock, and Binky knew who she was when I told them that I did her make-up for her video. Her career was really on the rise and I was going right with her. *I can't do this with Boss.* I told him he had to get some help. I always dealt with the drug dealer, not the addict. This is a whole new world to me.

CHAPTER 35

THE SET UP

"What's the word Moose?" The clock was ticking and my time was winding down. *North Carolina here I come to meet the Diamond.*

"Well I found out that Lala is working with Sweets. Somehow she's been supplying us through Sweets."

"What the fuck? How is that even possible? That's what that bitch meant when she said I was still paying her! Man, I need for you to explain this shit. I left that up to you and Jock to handle."

"You didn't leave it up to me; you left it up to Jock. I guess whoever he had running for him was doing it on the sneak tip." *Moose is full of shit, that's not how Jock carried it.*

"No, Jock always dealt with the supplier first-hand. He never had any third party running for him. You know damn well these suppliers don't even work like that! They are not dealing with any new faces; they will blow your brains out first."

"My point exactly! Which brings me to the reason why Jock was killed in the first place. I think he tried it without letting us in on his plans, so he was used as an example." *I hear what Moose is saying but it's not making sense. Jock wouldn't do that. I need to talk to Jock's uncle and see why he stopped supplying us in the first place. To my knowledge, stuff got too hot for him.*

"They wouldn't have put his head on the trunk of my car. Okay, whatever. Let's just move on from this scenario. I'm going to take care of Lala tonight. She won't exist in a minute, so she's no longer going to be a part of the equation."

"Yeah, you should have taken care of that when you had a chance."

"Moose, you know it don't work like that. Before I could get out the car good enough I heard sirens and I'm rolling with a gun, it was time to pull away and get lost. Here you not thinking again, I would have been locked up. I'm not trying to go be locked the fuck up."

"Yeah, you right, I wasn't thinking. I'm just ready for all this shit to be over with."

"Did you do what I asked you to do?"

"Yeah, the meet is going down at that old warehouse behind Old Town at six o'clock. They think that they're meeting with a new supplier that will give Sweets a better deal. I have everyone lined up in place. I also have the same deal set up for Rock. Now, you already know that everybody is going to bring their right hand men with them for safety."

"That's what we want; take them all out at once. Are you sure that you have the whole building covered? Parked cars loaded up all over the place in hidden spots? We need a little bit of light traffic walking that direction. Some dudes playing craps for a good fake out."

"I have everything covered. Man, you know me! I've been on it all week long!"

"Moose, we can't have no fuck ups. Everything has to go our way in order for this to work. Who do you have in place as the fake supplier?"

"This cat from New York; he knows what to do. He's bringing a few of his men; believe me I have every crack covered. Your back is covered. We're going in separately. You go in the front and I'm coming in from the back. We will give them five minutes. The boys will give us the signal from the roof."

"Alright, I will meet up with you there. Remember Moose, we are doing this for Jock, everybody has to go down." I gave Moose dap as we parted ways until the meet.

"Oh I'm ready best believe it, make no mistakes about it!" Moose was assuring me.

As I was driving I was concentrating on making sure all the boys were in place. There were five parked cars in place just like I asked. I saw the guys lying down on the roof. When I pulled up and looked over to my left, I saw Moose across the street. Moose had been sitting there since noon watching the ins and outs. He said he saw everybody go in so far except Rock. *He must be running late or he's already in there and Moose didn't see him.* I parked the car, got out, opened my trunk, grabbed the trash bag and threw it over my back as a little distraction. I walked on the side of the building and threw my mask on. Once I got the signal from Moose that it was a go, I headed on in the warehouse as planned, strapped from top to bottom so when one gun ran out of bullets I had the other. *I shouldn't need that much ammunition especially with all the boys in place.* As soon as I stepped foot in the warehouse, I heard the click from the guns. It felt like two of them were pointed at the back of my head. *I feel like I'm a dead man. I should have left when Diamond said leave.* I looked straight ahead and there goes Sweets and Rock on the ground with guns pointed to their heads. *I already know what this is. The feds got all of us, but where the fuck is Moose? He never came in from that back door.*

*****

"You ready to take this shit over?" Moose asked.

"Yes, I'm assuming everything went as planned?" Lala smiled. "Let's go!"

Other Books by Stacey Fenner

A Toxic Love Affair
Available at: Amazon

Tyrone and Daniel are two best friends but total opposites. Tyrone has his woman at home taking care of the kids while he's out playing in the streets. He soon finds out that being too comfortable and secure will cost him everything when he comes home to an empty home.

Will his womanizing ways wreck his life or can he get it together before it's to late?

Daniel on the other hand, is still trying to heal from a messy divorce with Candace five years later. He's tried dating but finds it hard to move on.

Find out what happens with a good-looking man who has money to buy everything but is unfulfilled on the inside. A Toxic Love Affiar is filled with love, lust, hate and drama.

*****

A Toxic Love Affair 2
Available at: Amazon

They say once a good girl is gone she's gone forever, and if you thought Part 1 threw you for a loop, then get ready to do figure 8's this go around.

Belinda sets out on a mission to destroy all her childhood, so-called, friends that have betrayed her. She has no boundaries or limits to her destruction. She has intentions on making each and every one of them pay, and has masterminded a plan that will eventually cause her to self-destruct in the worst way!

Being disloyal to Belinda will cost them everything. Everybody likes to play but nobody wants to pay!

Meanwhile, Daniel finally opens himself up to love again after going through his messy divorce with his scandalous ex-wife, Candace. That won't last too long when a jealous Candace gets wind of the relationship; she throws a monkey wrench trying to exhaust him of all hope. Meanwhile, Daniel is stuck cleaning up the mess Tyrone created.

Find out if Tyrone and Daniel's friendship can survive the aftermath when Daniel gets wind to what Belinda is up to and he feels responsible for her trifling ways. Shocked is an understatement as to how he feels about a woman he once had so much respect for.

Read and see just how toxic these relationships become!

About Stacey Fenner

Instagram: authorstaceyfenner
Twitter: sfenner1
Facebook: www.facebook.com/authorstaceyfenner

You can contact Stacey Fenner at
authorstaceyfenner@gmail.com

Stacey Fenner, was born December 1 and raised in New Haven, CT., the youngest of three. In 1999 Stacey relocated to Atlanta, GA where she resided for a year before moving to Baltimore, MD to care for her parents with her two daughters.

Writing since she was a child was a way to express herself, allowing her to overcome many trials and tribulations. However, she never pursued her gift until 2008. Although she obtained her degree in accounting, and currently works in that field, her passion is and always has been writing.

Stacey's writing career is focused upon novels about relationships. Her first book, A Toxic Love Affair, which was published in April of 2015, landed her in the #37 spot on the Woman's Urban Best Selling list. Her follow-up novel, A Toxic Love Affair Part 2, landed in the # 24 spot on that very same list. Having just recently finished up Part 3 of that series, Stacey is taking the Indie world by storm.